Divine Comedy

Spiritual Musings & Hysterical Religious Cartoons

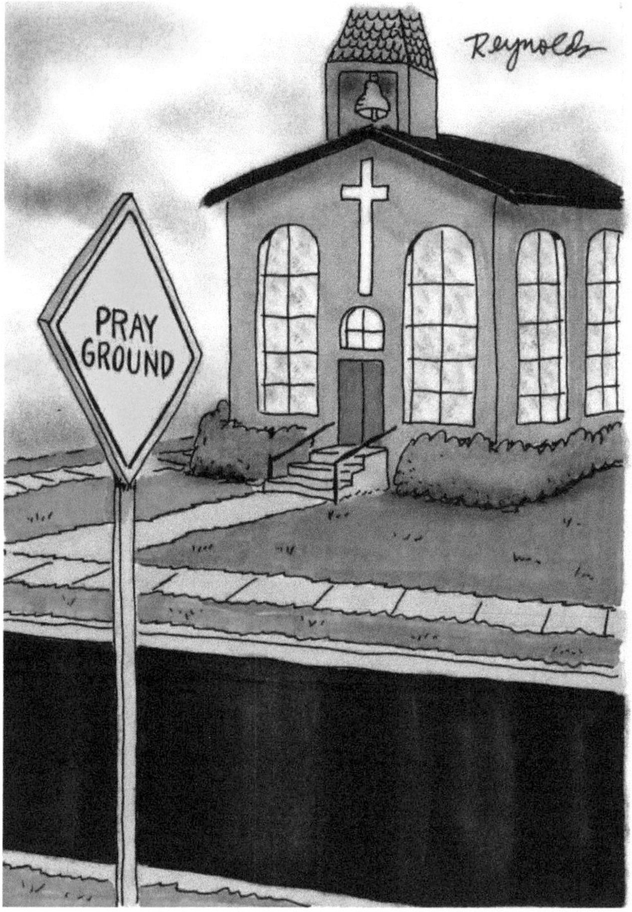
Reynolds
PRAY
GROUND

Dan Reynolds

Joseph Weiss, Editor

SmartAsk Books
Rancho Santa Fe, California, USA
www.smartaskbooks.com

ISBN-13: 978-1-943760-93-0 (Color Print)
ISBN-13: 978-1-943760-94-7 (e-Book)

FOREWORD

Being funny is an area that many people strive for and not all succeed in. Dan Reynolds is an example of a man who has mastered the art of humor and can display it on a consistent basis, as exemplified by his thousands of cartoons. As a man who has been creating new masterpieces for 28 years and counting, Dan knows a thing or two about creating cartoons, and has been the face behind greeting cards that you yourself have probably bought without knowing that he created it.

He has drawn humor (no pun intended) from even the most monotonous of places. With such a wide variety of topics covered throughout his cartooning career, it is next to impossible to find a cartoon that you cannot relate to in some way, shape, or form.

Living with him my whole life gives me an exclusive look at how his humor has developed and how it plays out throughout each day. I am blessed to have a man like him as my father. He has proved that he is much more than just a cartoonist, but an overall great guy and amazing dad. He is truly a man that everyone can look up to, and a staple for those looking for humor.

- Jimmy Reynolds
(Dan's youngest son)

creator Instagram's
@litcatholicmemes

Reynolds

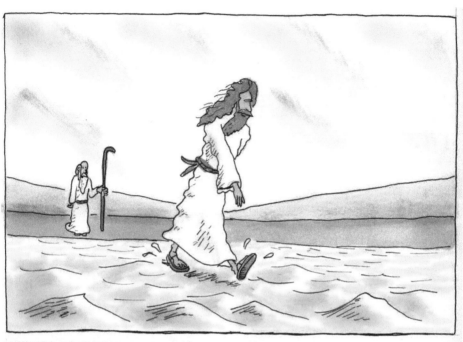

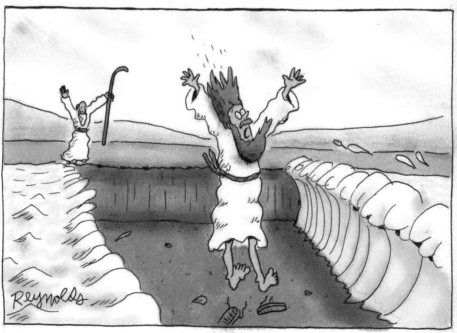

The Church becomes family
when the family
comes to church.

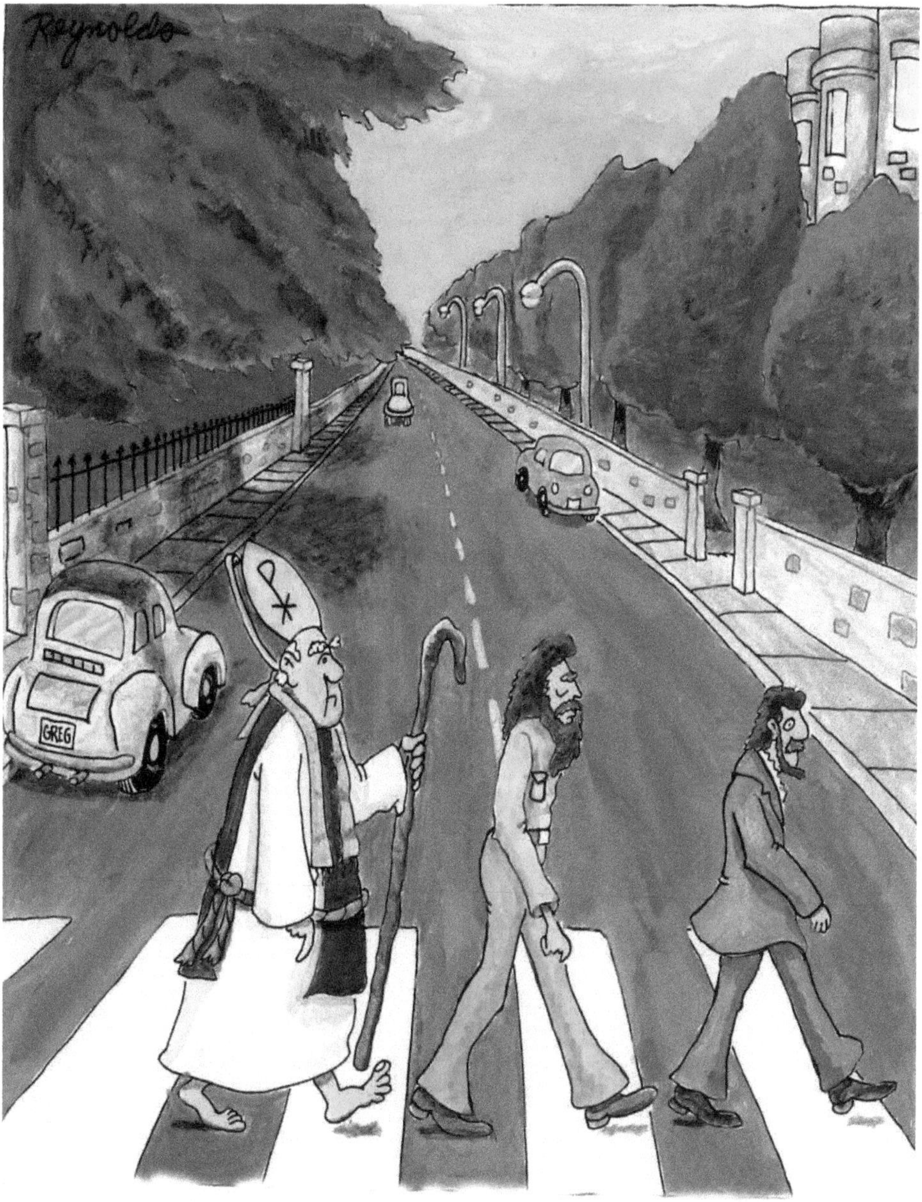
Reynolds
GREG

John Paul, George, and Ringo

God gives us His Mercy. We should give Him our 'Merci'.

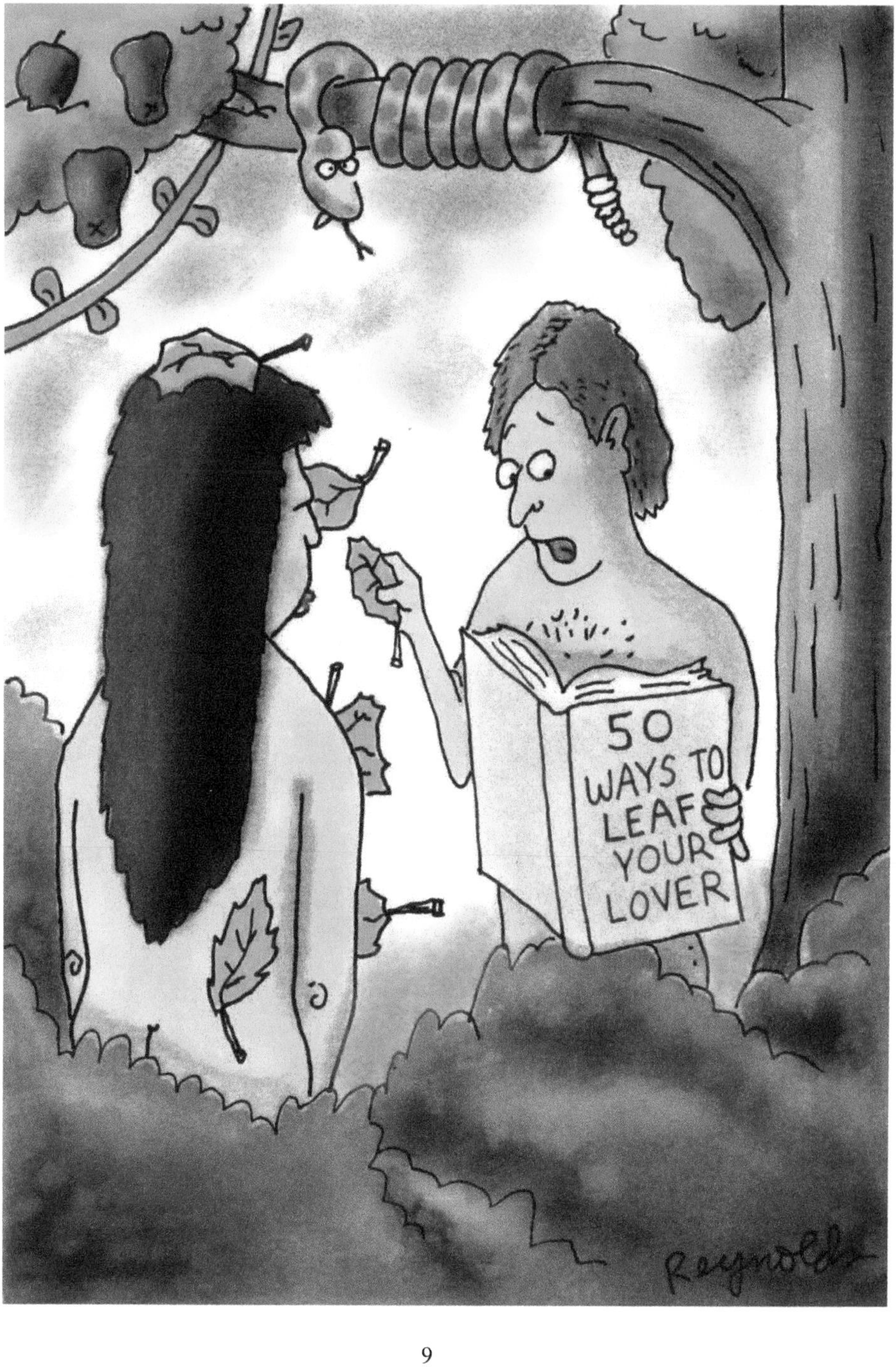
50 WAYS TO LEAF YOUR LOVER
Reynolds

Remember, no matter how dark your night, the "Son" is risen.

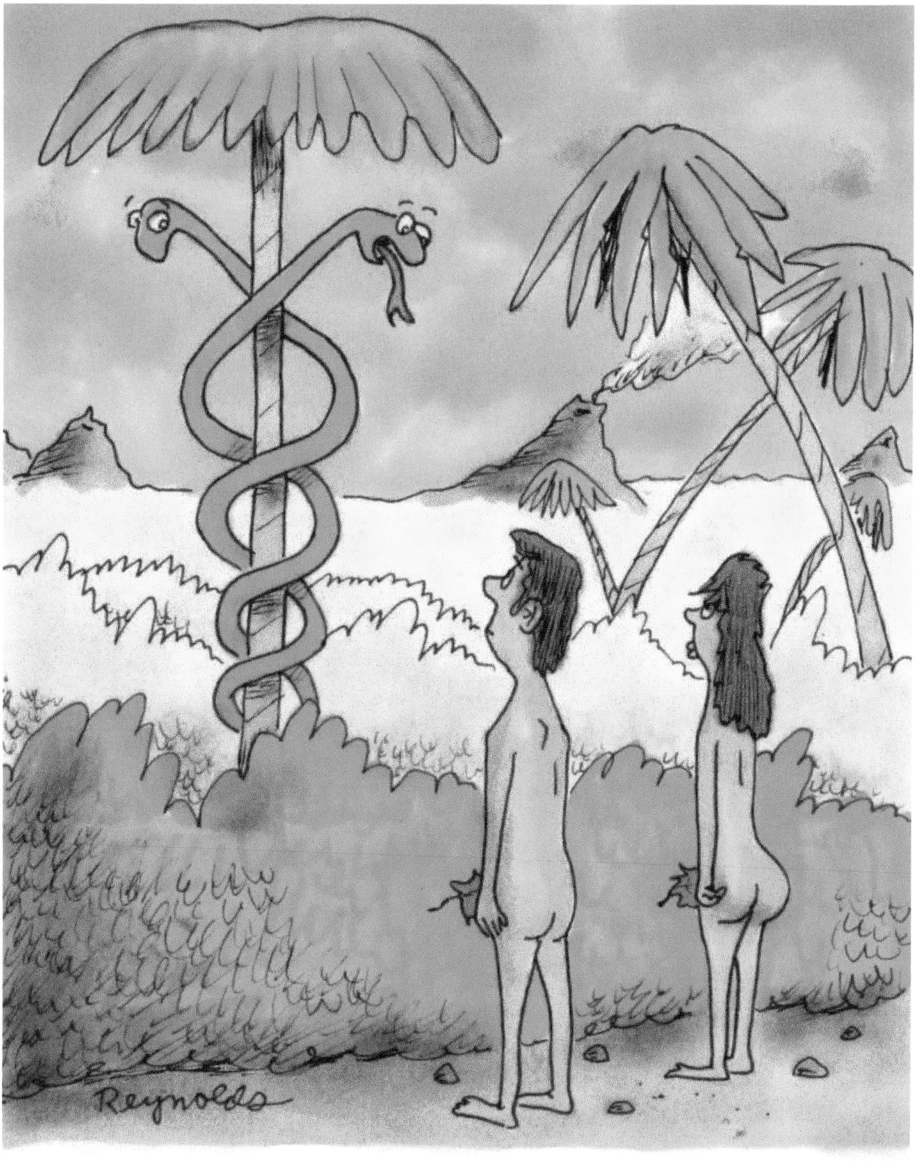
Reynolds

"The Tree of Knowledge is down the road. This is the Tree of Affordable Health Insurance."

When we say the most important thing in life is love, we are admitting, that God is the most important thing in life because "God IS Love."

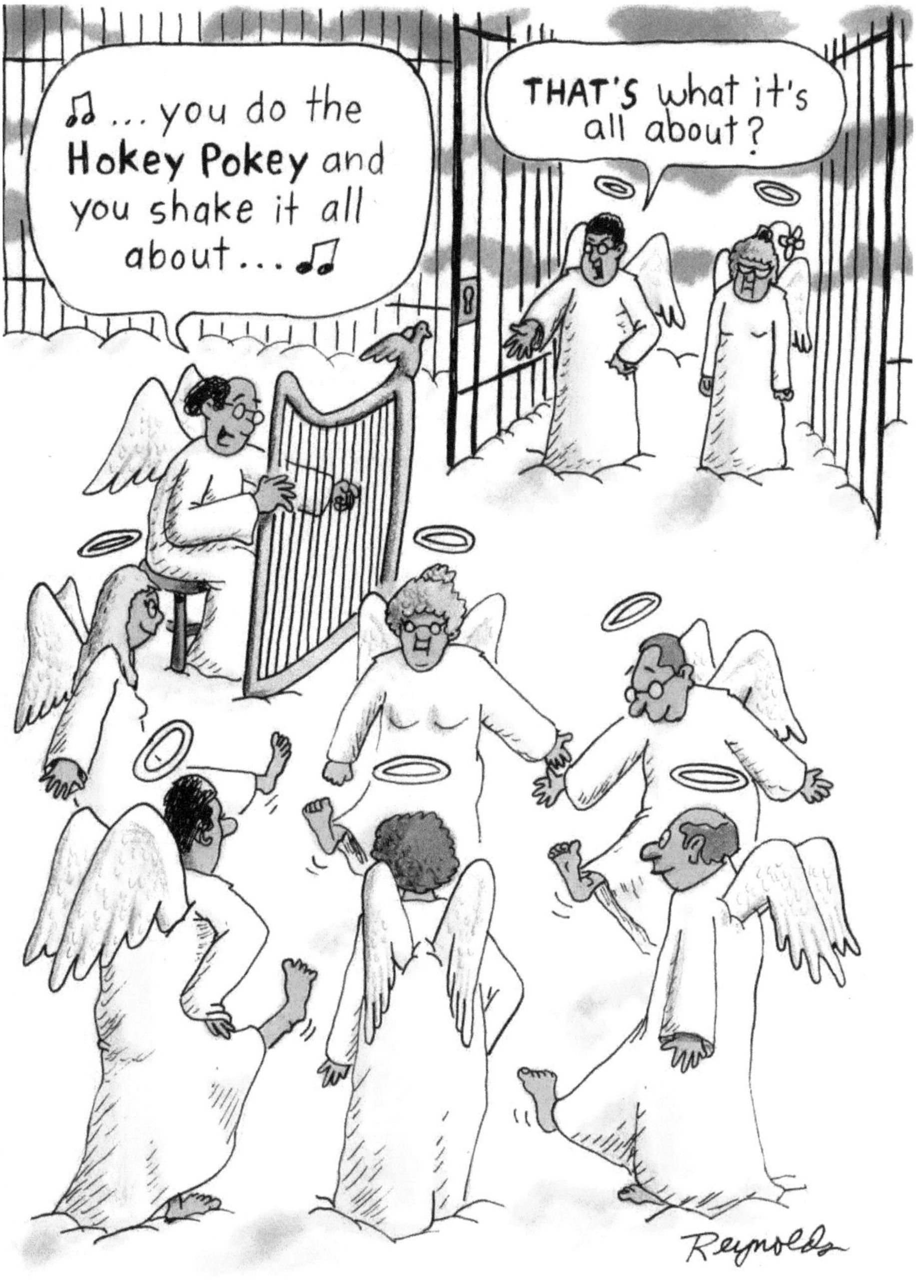
♫ ...you do the **Hokey Pokey** and you shake it all about... ♫
THAT'S what it's all about?
Reynolds

When life brings you walls,
God builds you bridges.

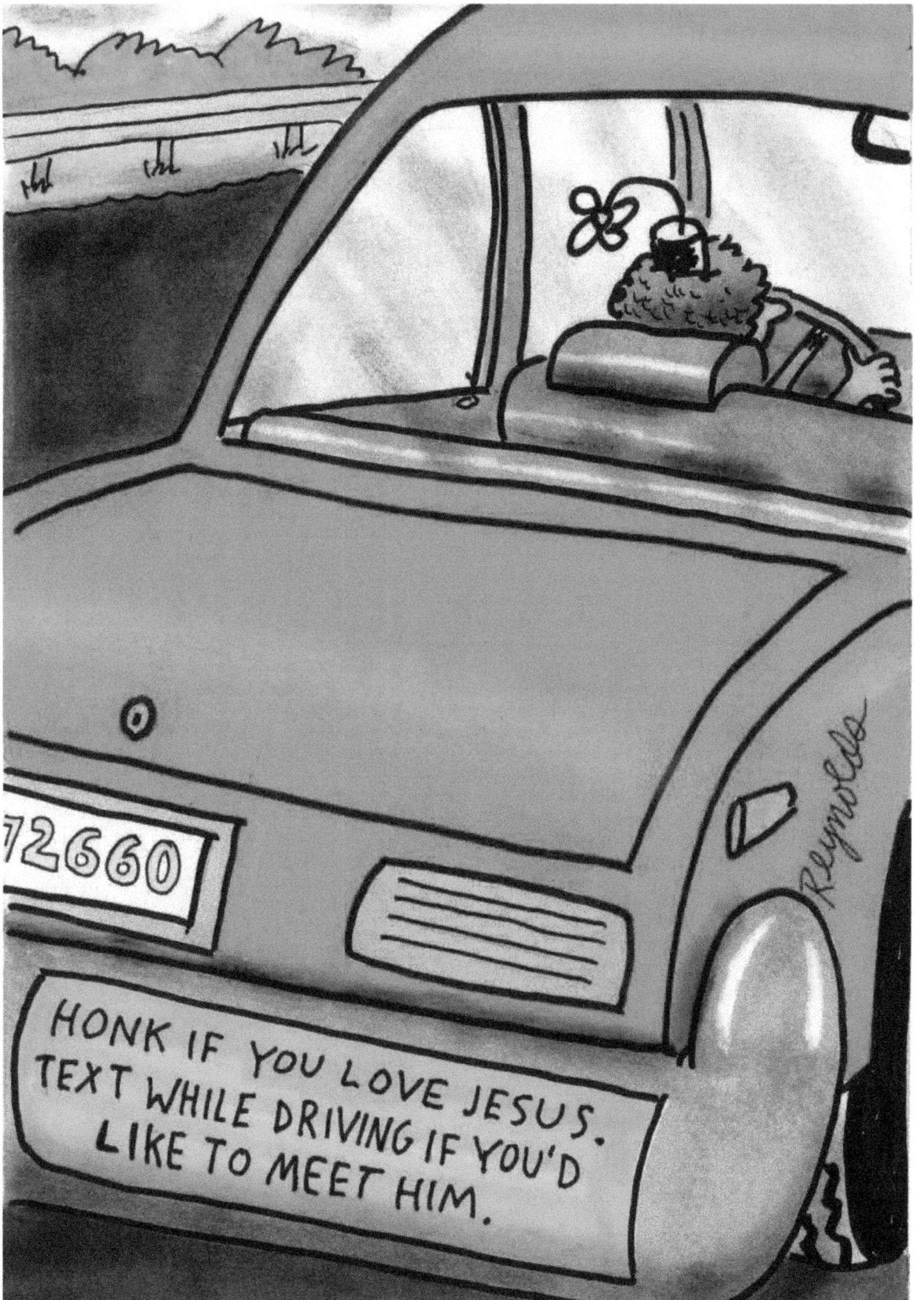
72660
HONK IF YOU LOVE JESUS.
TEXT WHILE DRIVING IF YOU'D LIKE TO MEET HIM.
Reynolds

God made laughter as necessary to life as water. That's why He named it: "H_2O H_2O H_2O".

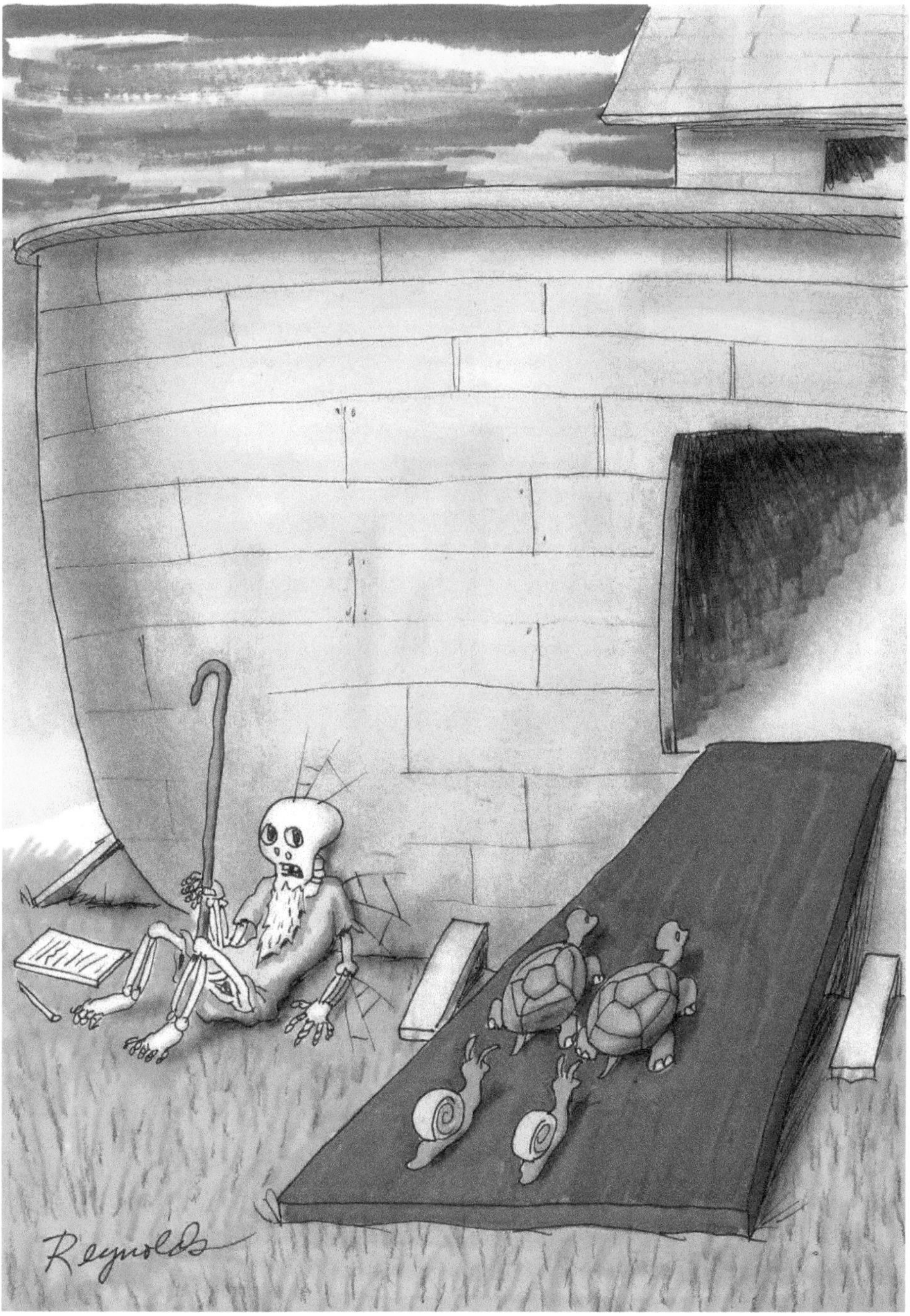
Reynolds

Just because God took Sunday off when He created the world, doesn't mean you get to take the day off from church.

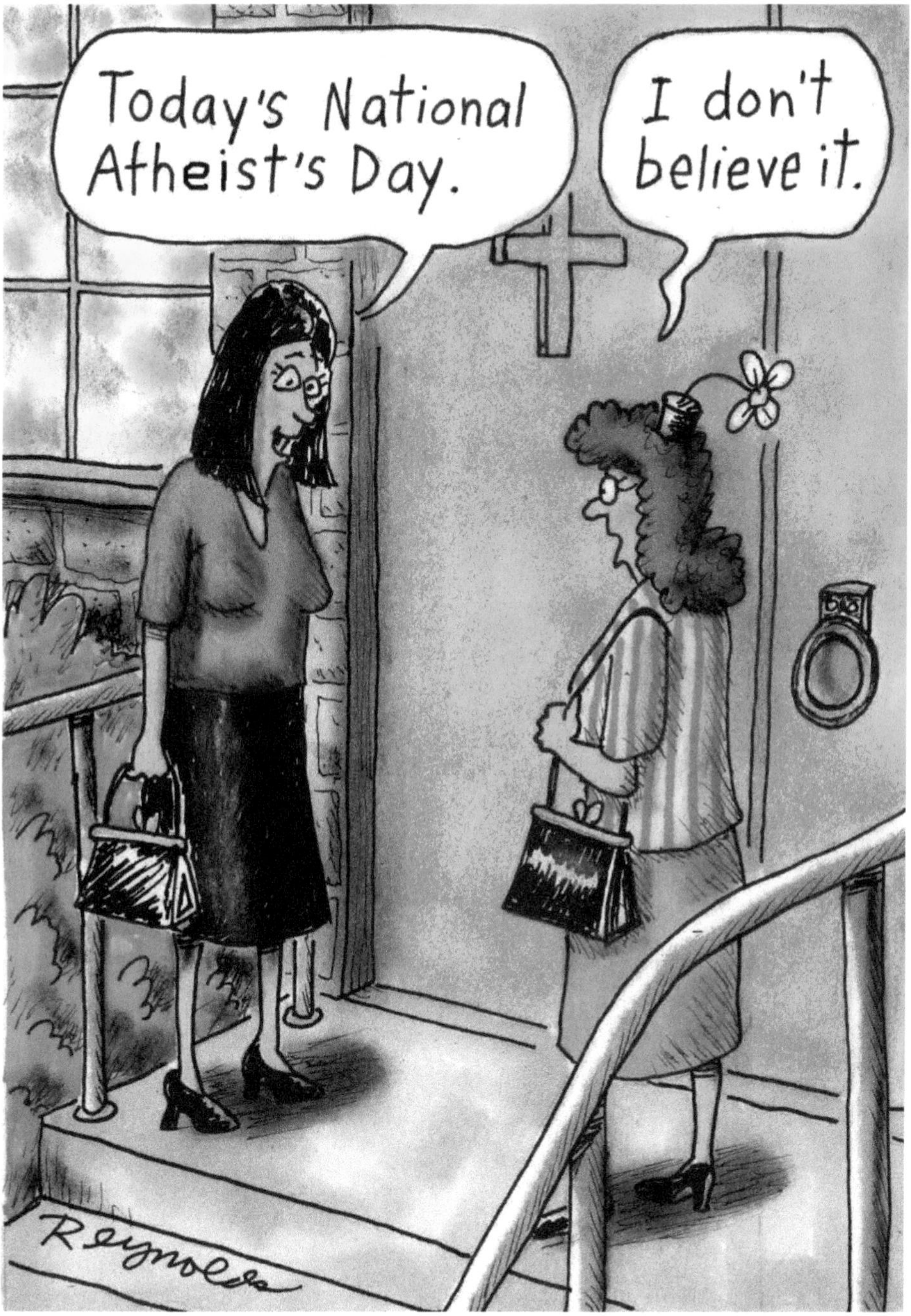
Today's National Atheist's Day.
I don't believe it.
Reynolds

Descartes said, "I think, therefore, I am." God says, "I AM; therefore, you think."

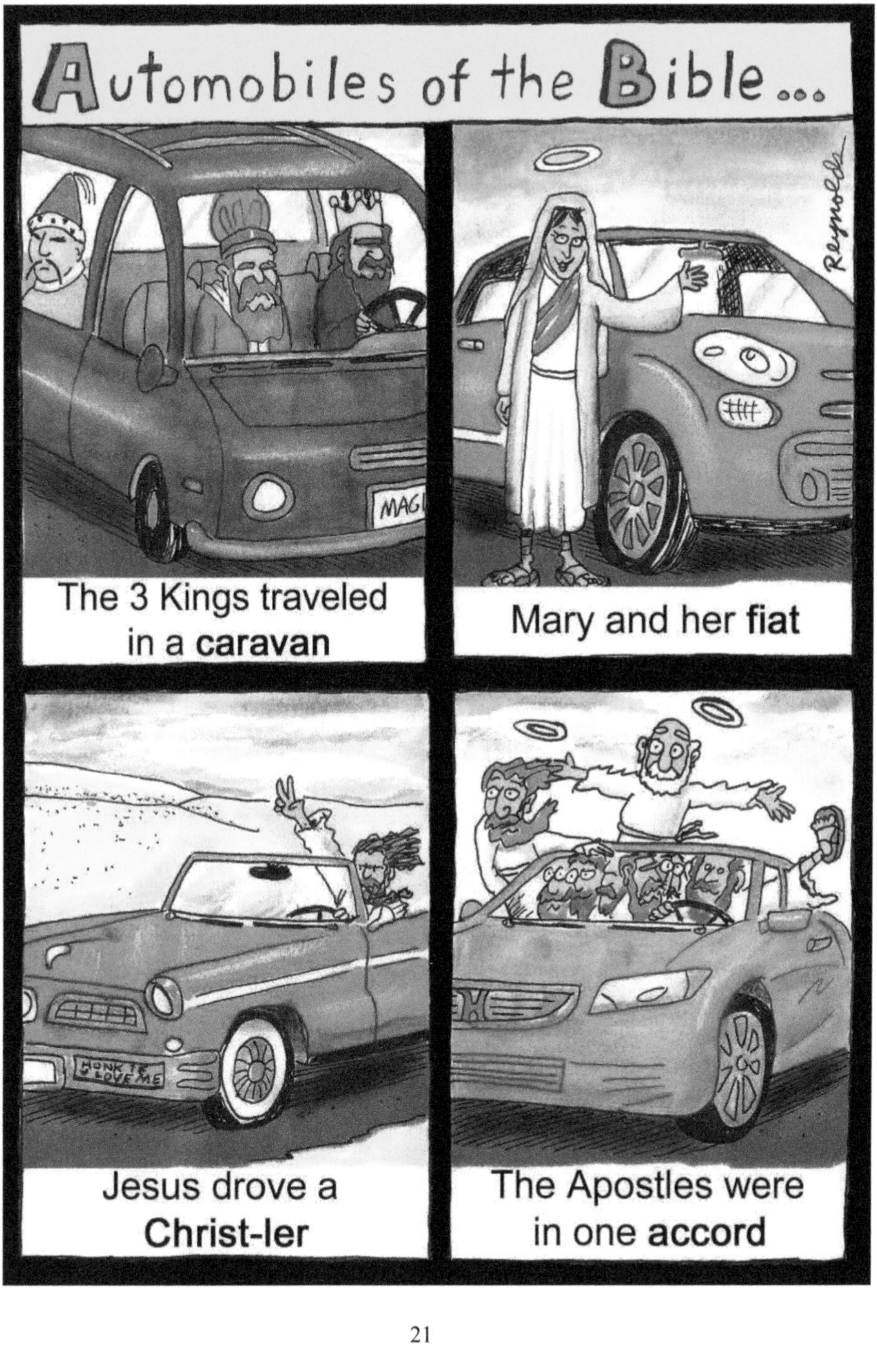
Automobiles of the Bible...
Reynolds
MAG
The 3 Kings traveled in a caravan
Mary and her fiat
Jesus drove a Christ-ler
The Apostles were in one accord

When you feel lost and say, "Lord, I can't find You", turn around, He'll be found, standing directly behind you.

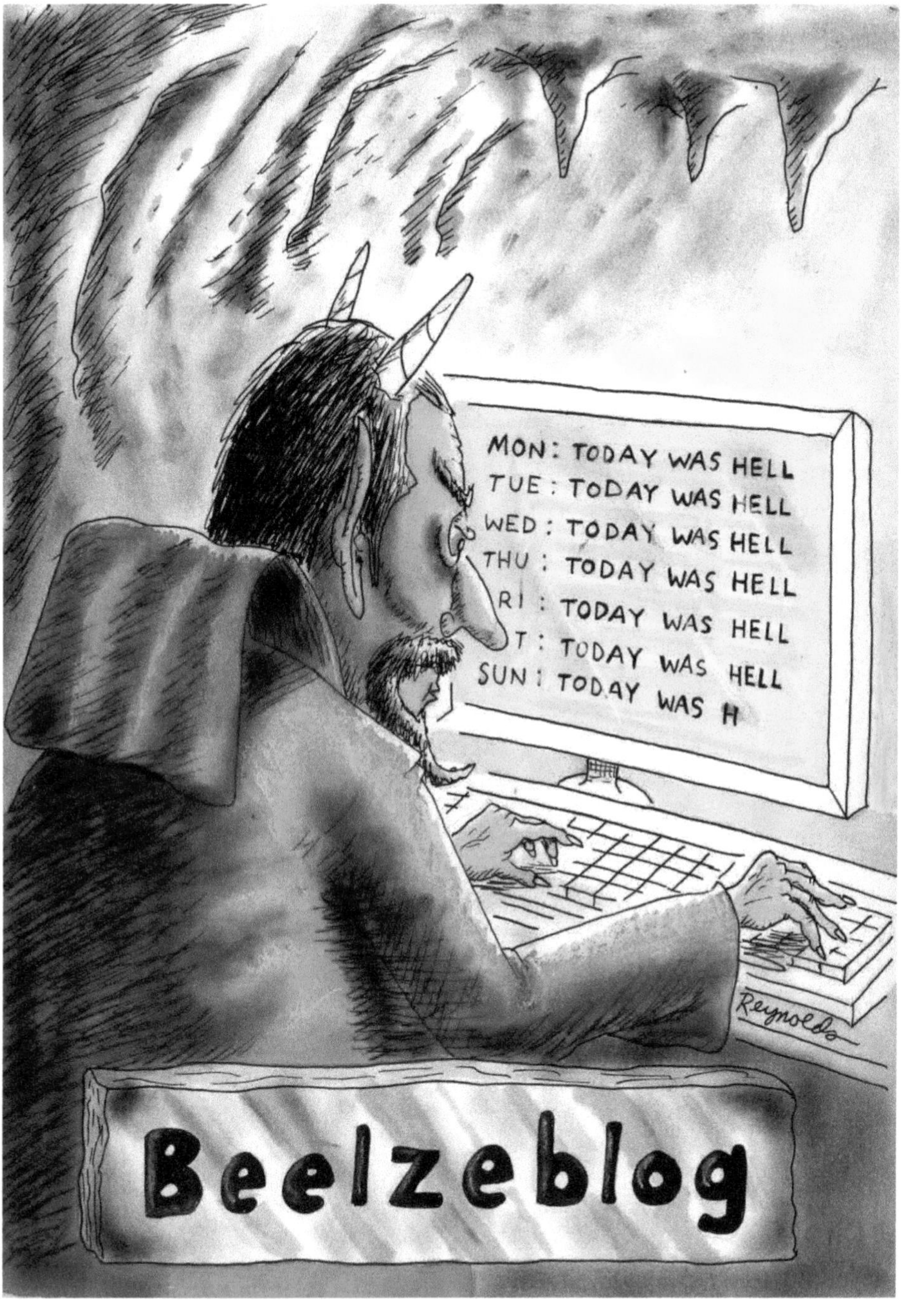
MON: TODAY WAS HELL
TUE : TODAY WAS HELL
WED : TODAY WAS HELL
THU : TODAY WAS HELL
RI : TODAY WAS HELL
T : TODAY WAS HELL
SUN : TODAY WAS H
Reynolds
Beelzeblog

In the Old Testament,
God said His name is
"I AM".
In the New Testament,
He finished His sentence
...... Love".

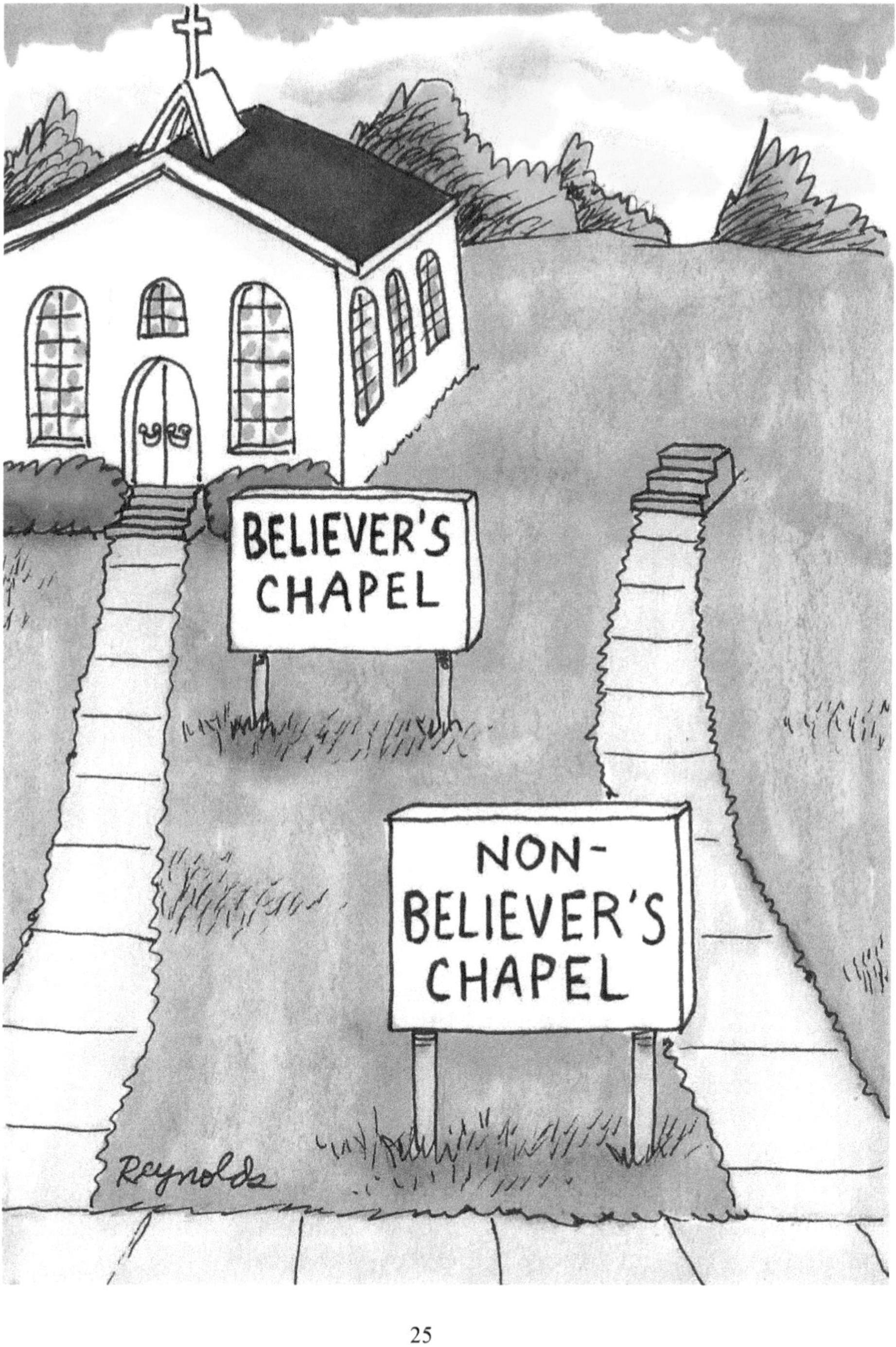
BELIEVER'S
CHAPEL
NON-
BELIEVER'S
CHAPEL
Reynolds

As a kid, I always thought if the Bible began with 'Genesis' ('Beginning'), then it should have ended with 'Exodus' ('Departure'), but then I had a 'Revelation'.

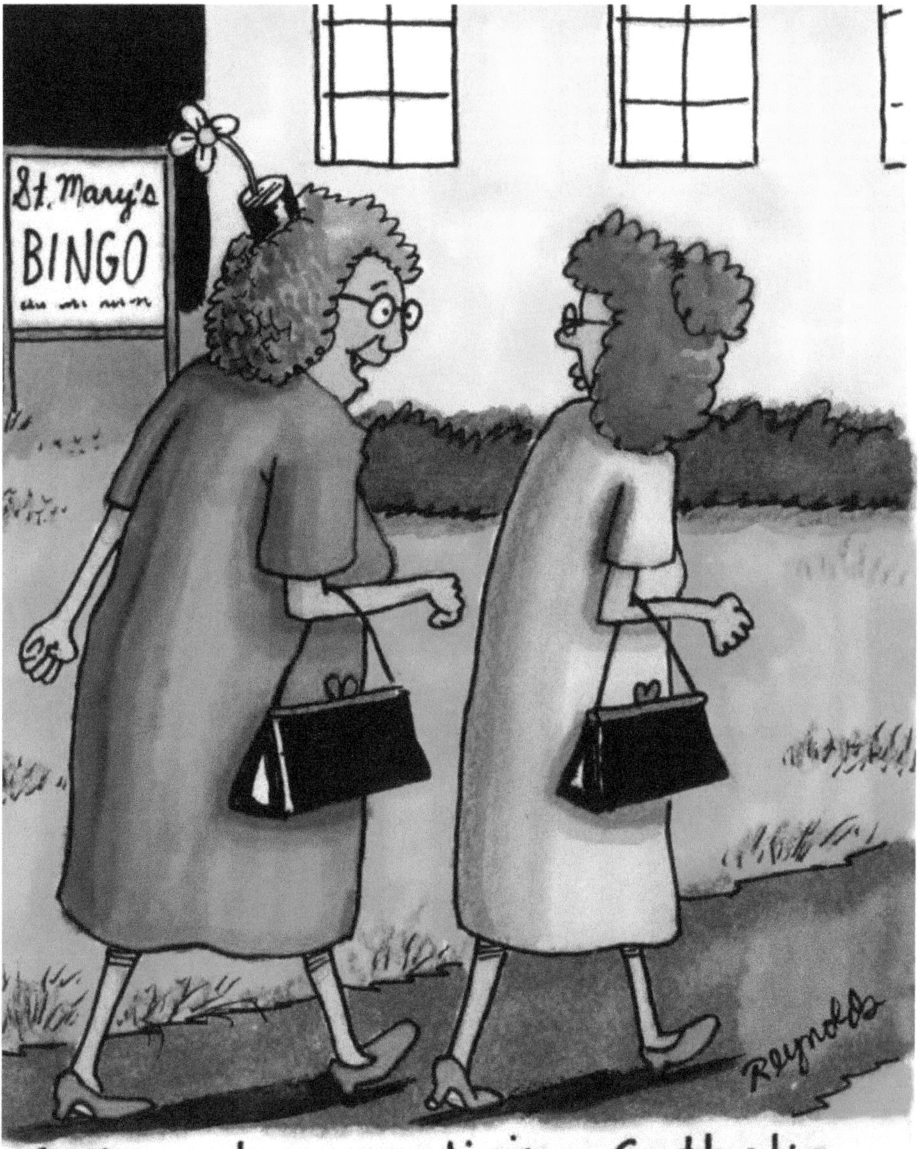
St. Mary's
BINGO
Reynolds

"I'm not a practicing Catholic anymore, but thanks to bingo I still get to church once a week."

God and science are not opposed. God created science. In fact, in order to create Eve from the rib, God had to split the first "Adam".

BINGO ADDICTS...

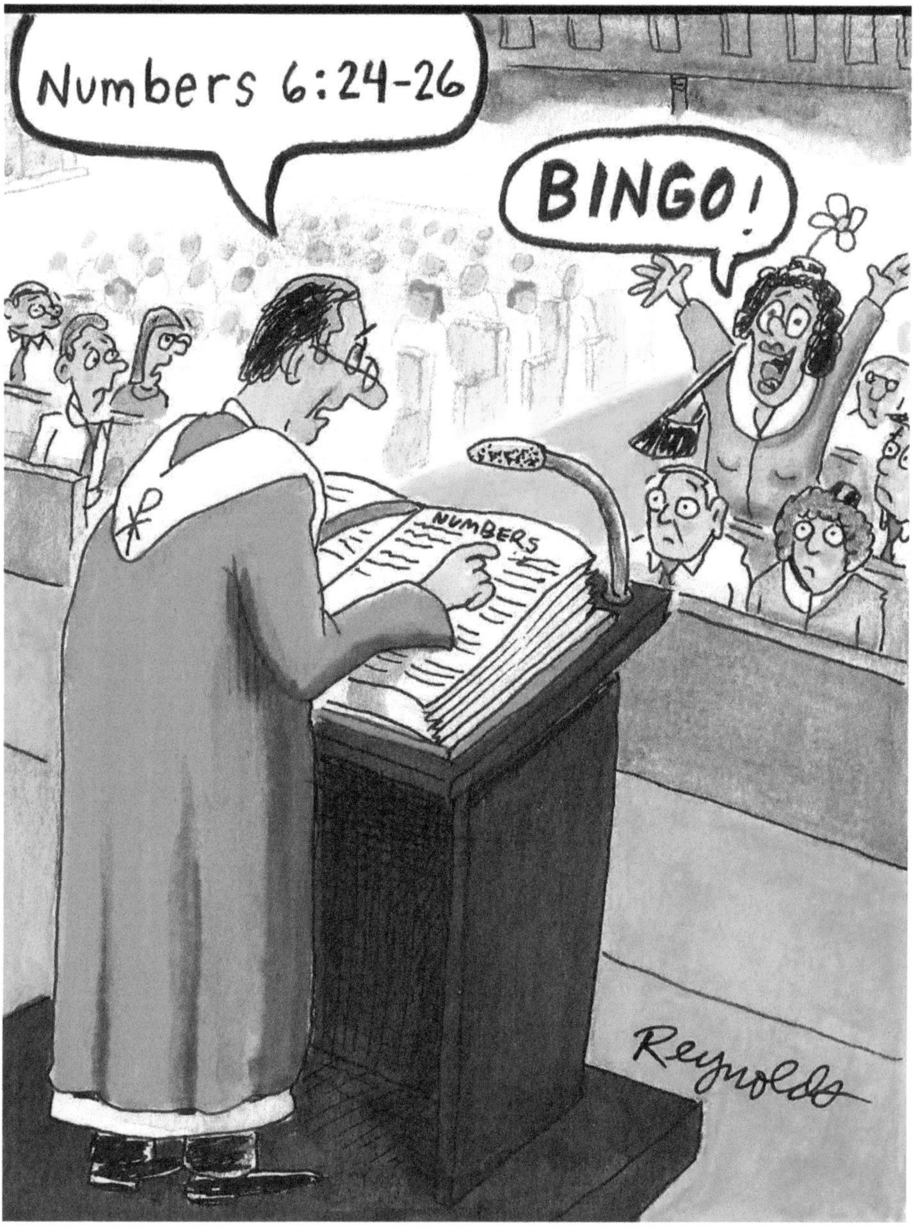
Numbers 6:24-26
BINGO!
NUMBERS
Reynolds

How does man give "praise" to God? The answer is in the question...He "prays".

Canary Heaven...

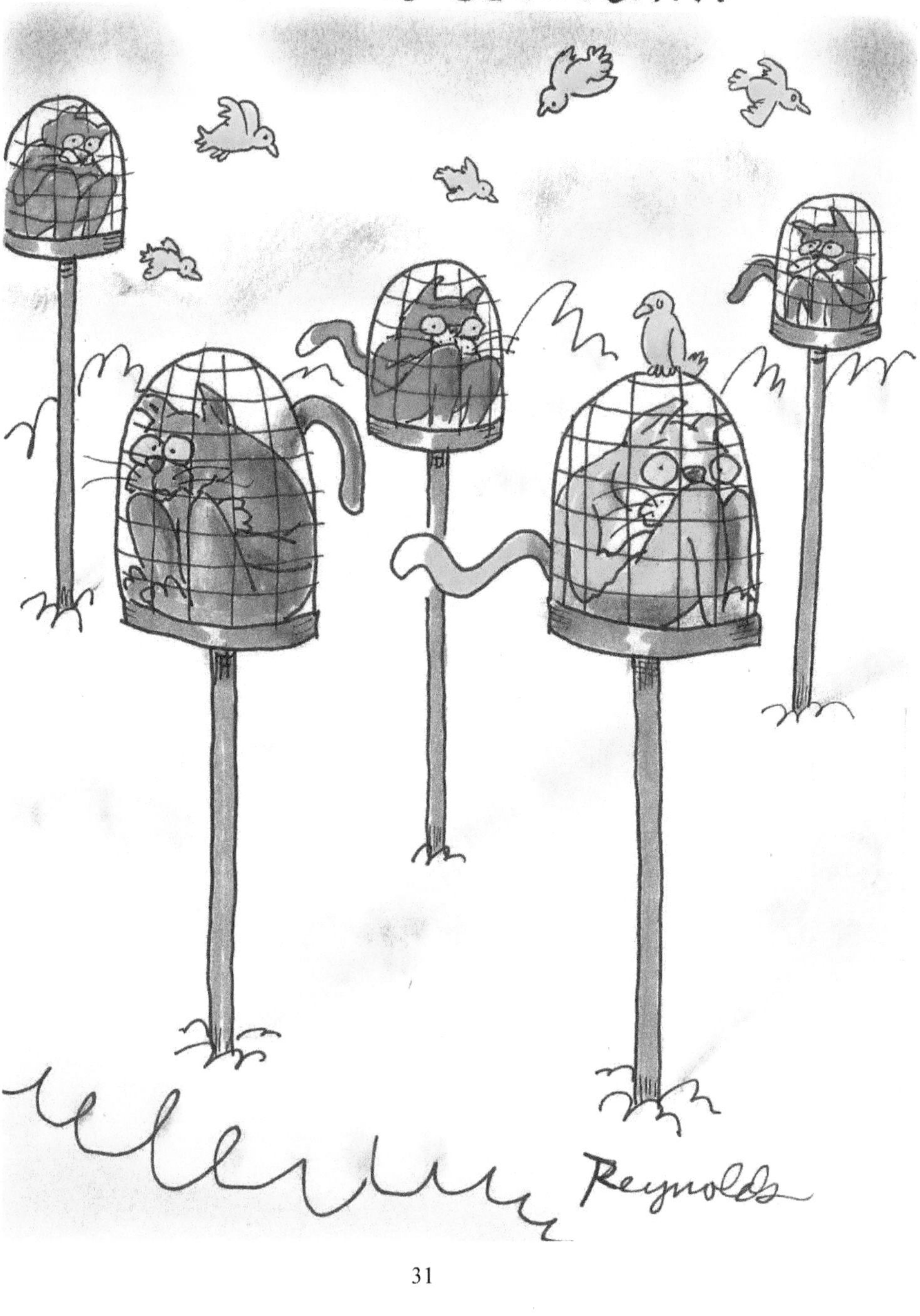
Reynolds

Jesus chose Peter to lead the Church so that we would be between a Rock and a heart place.

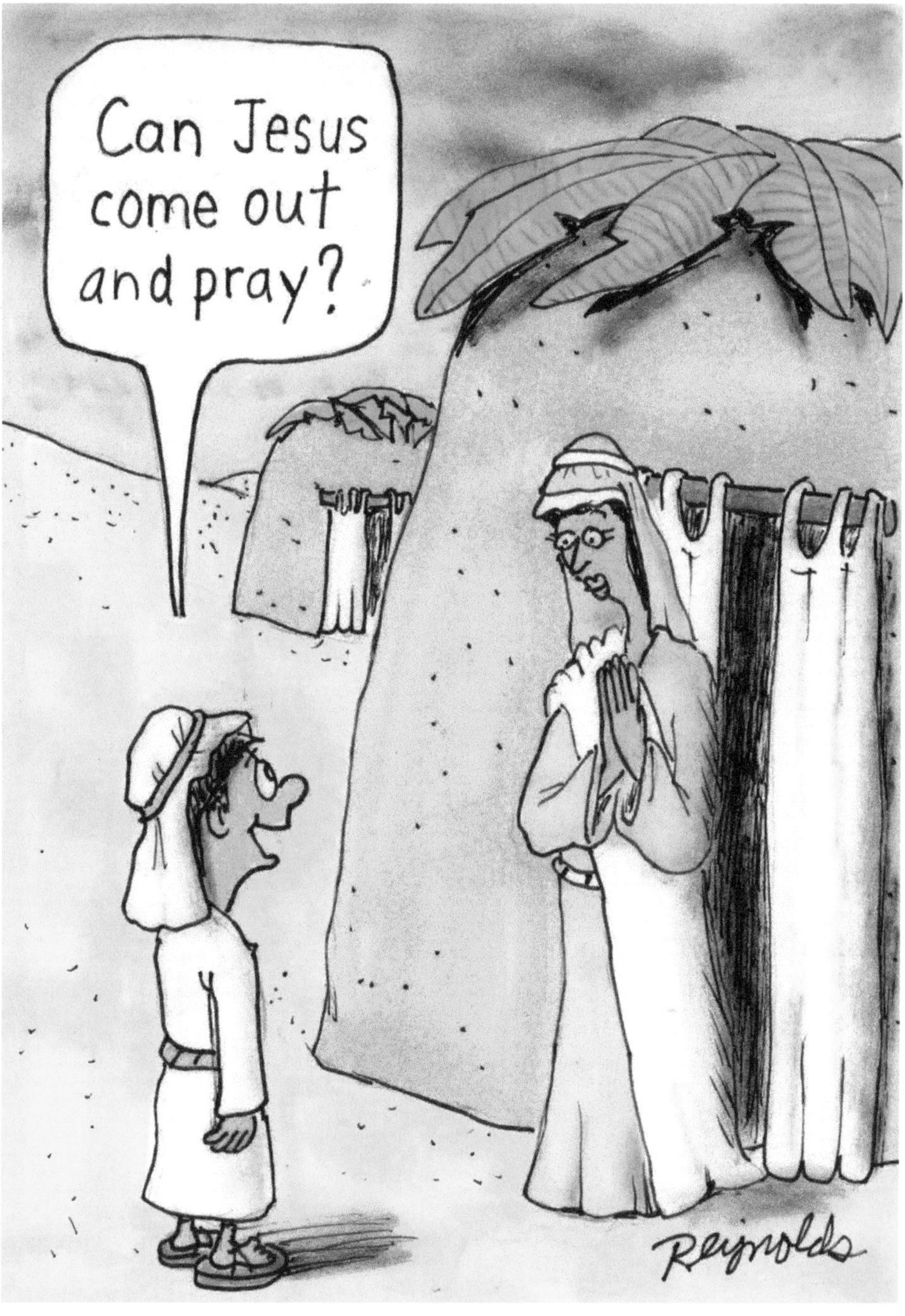
Can Jesus come out and pray?
Reynolds

God is merciful because He does not give us what we deserve. Instead, He gives us what we need.....
His Infinite Love.

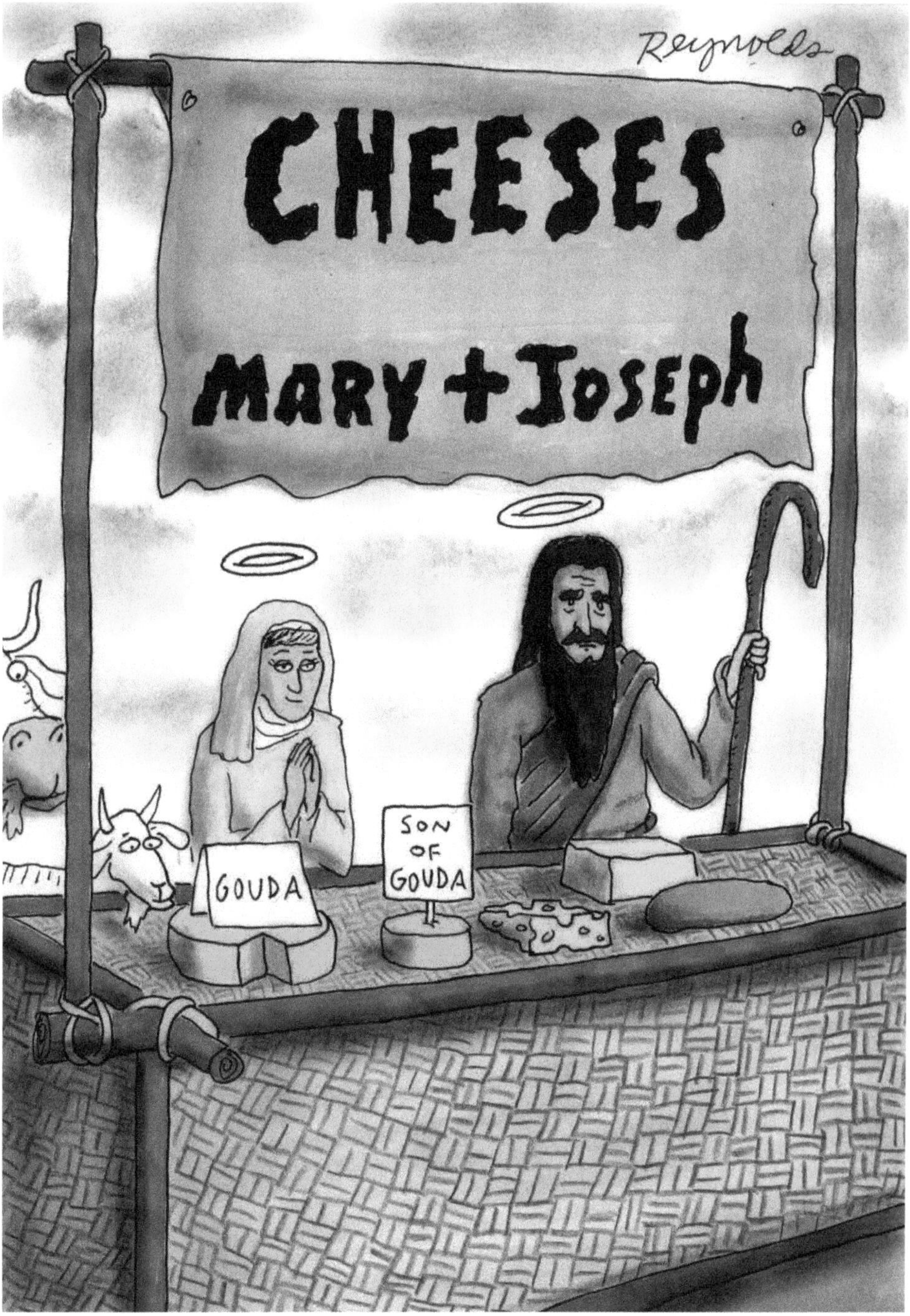
Reynolds
CHEESES
Mary + Joseph
SON
OF
GOUDA
GOUDA

When we speak, we
communicate reality as we
perceive it to another.
When God speaks,
He creates reality as it is
to all creation.

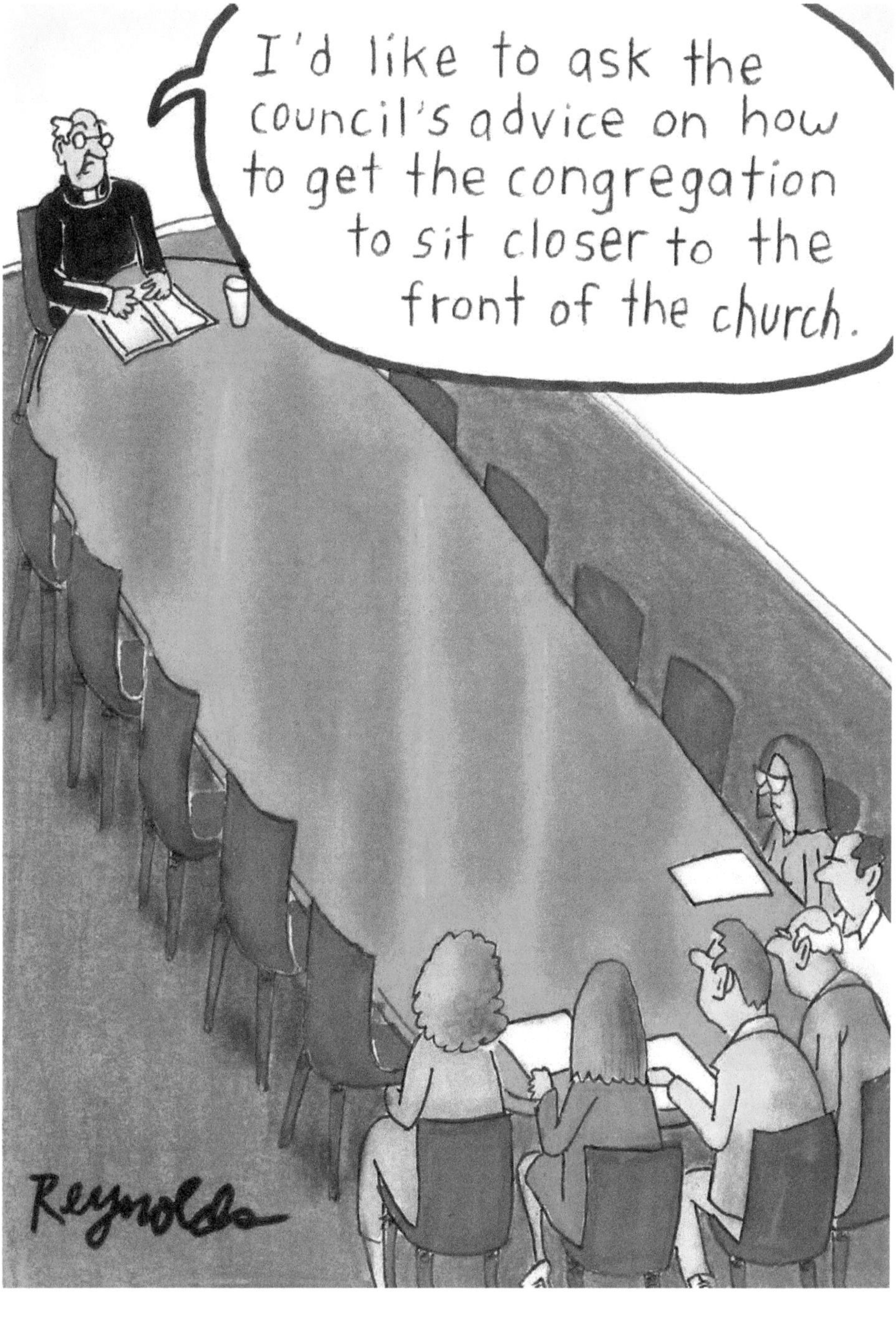
I'd like to ask the council's advice on how to get the congregation to sit closer to the front of the church.
Reynolds

Think of your life as a circle. Every time you walk away from God, you simultaneously are walking toward Him. Such is God's Infinite Mercy.

THE ORIGINAL GOOD CUP OF COFFEE...

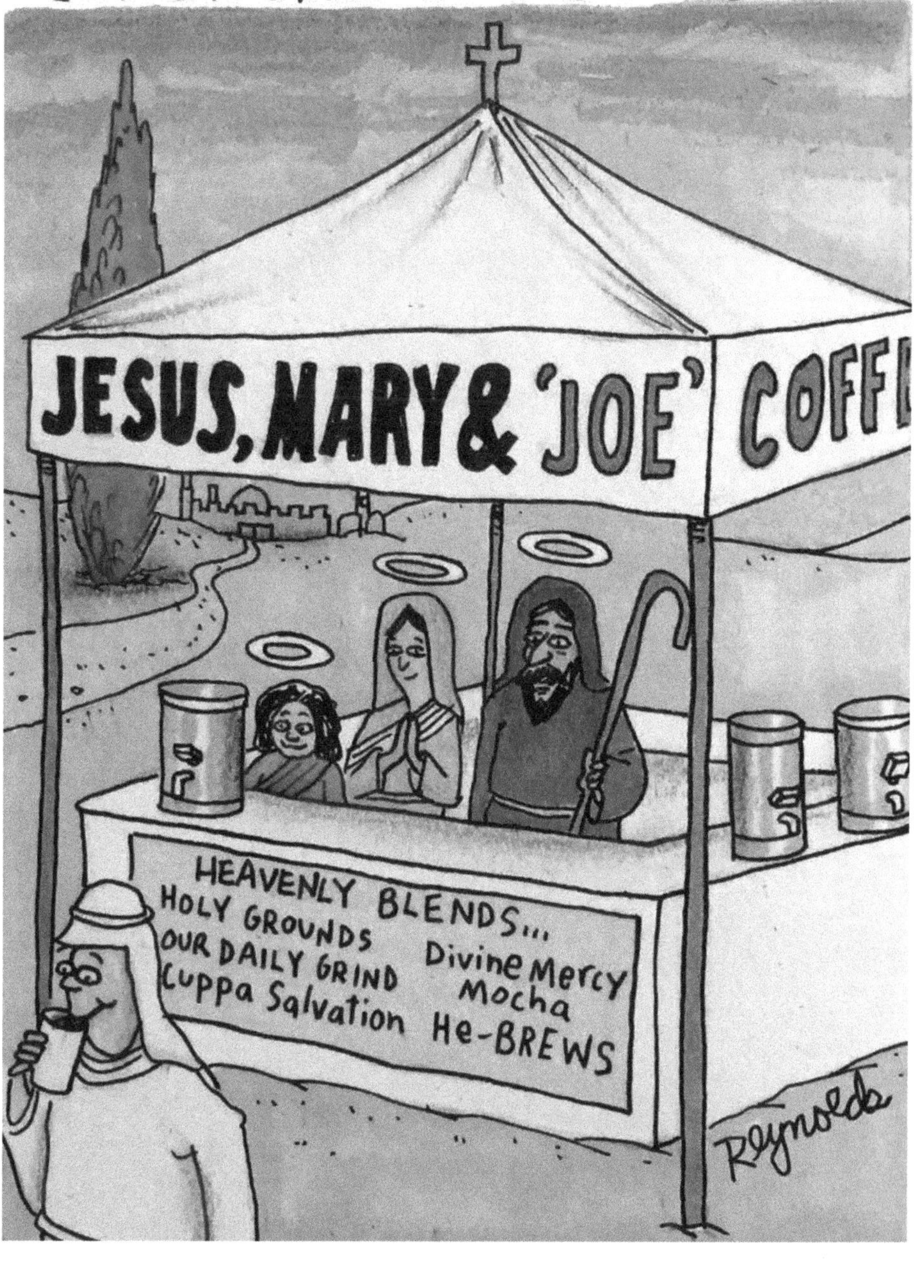

JESUS, MARY & 'JOE' COFF
HEAVENLY BLENDS...
HOLY GROUNDS
OUR DAILY GRIND
Cuppa Salvation
Divine Mercy Mocha
He-BREWS
Reynolds

Faith is not seeing the
unknown, it is knowing the
unseen. As soon as you
think you finally
understand God
you can be sure
you don't.

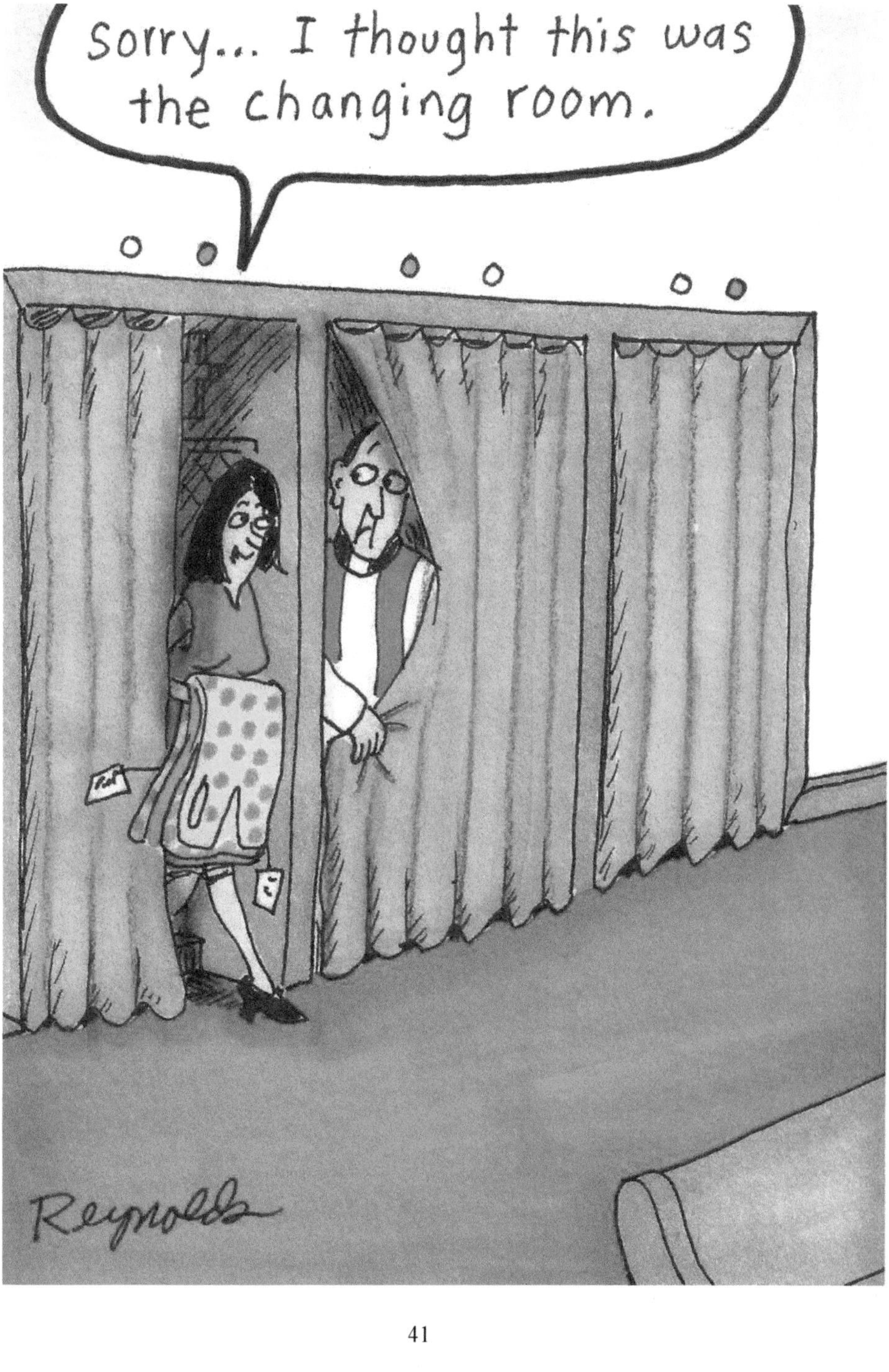
Sorry... I thought this was the changing room.
Reynolds

"Where there's a will,
there's a way", would be
better stated, "Where there's
God's Will,
there is 'The Way'."

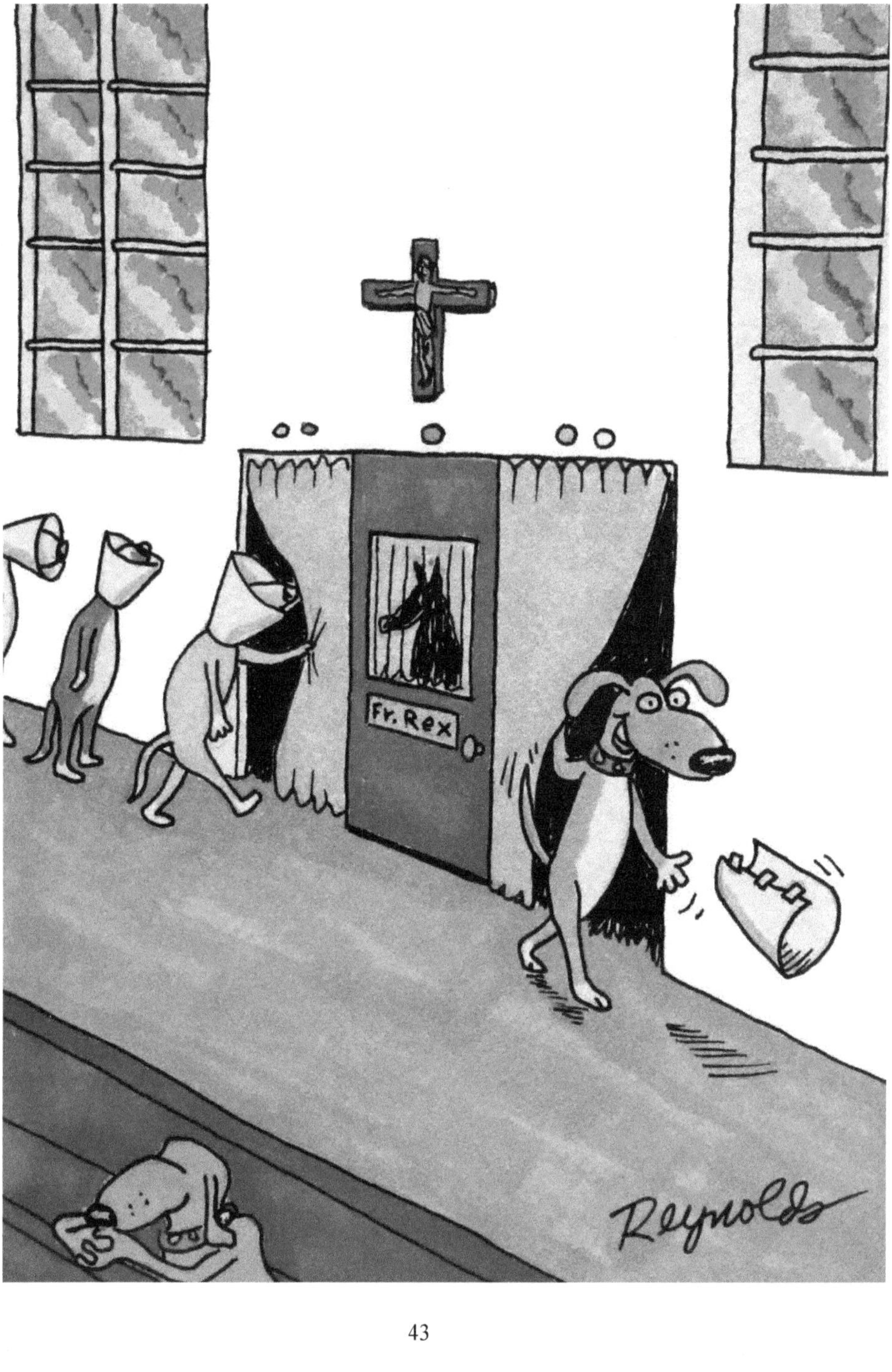
Fr. Rex
Reynolds

God is where the
"impossible" meets the
"I AM" possible.

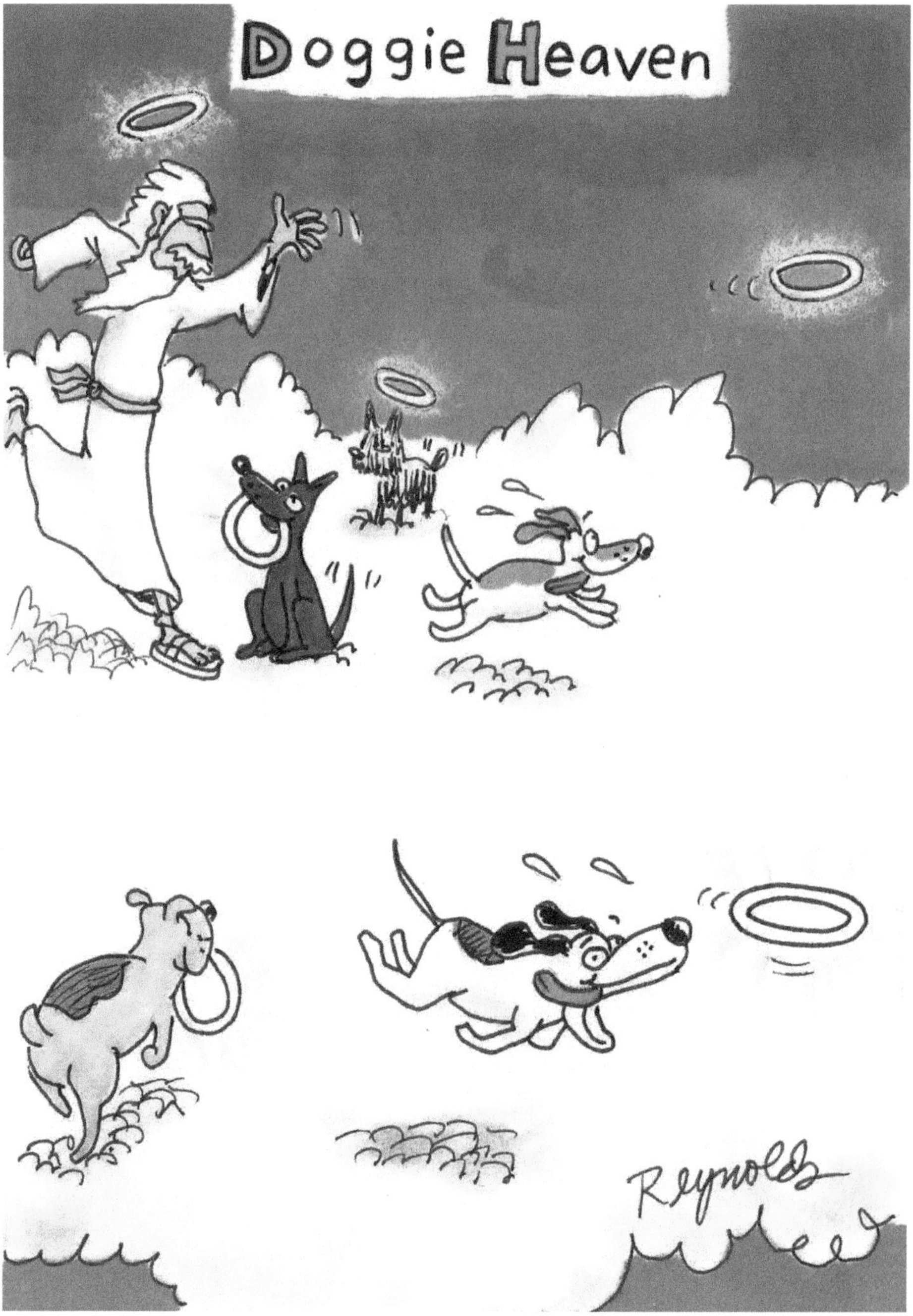
Doggie Heaven
Reynolds

If you get to know God,
you'll get to "No" Satan.

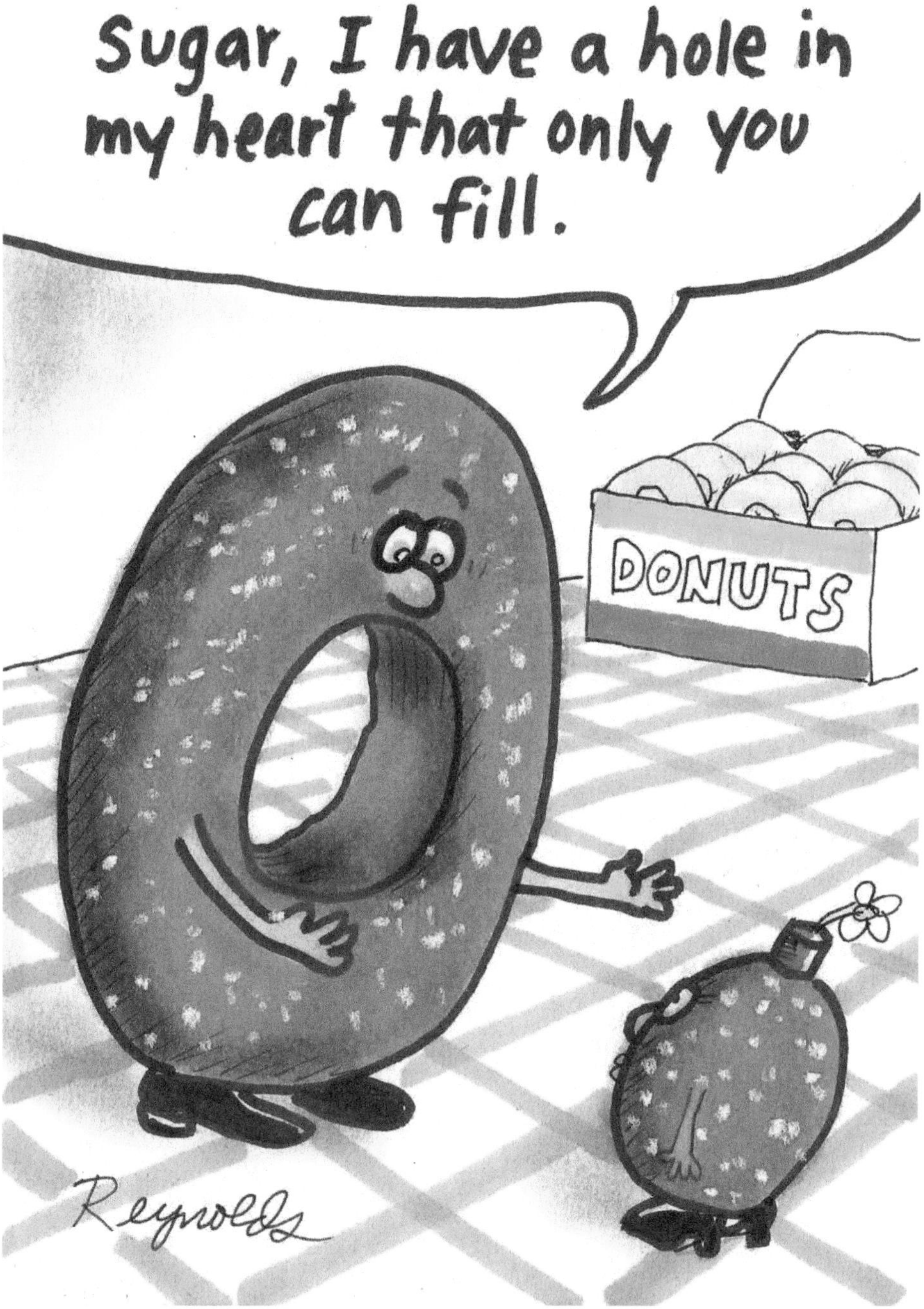
Sugar, I have a hole in my heart that only you can fill.
DONUTS
Reynolds

Miracles do not oppose the laws of nature. A miracle is a peak behind the curtain of supernatural truth from which the laws of nature themselves are born.

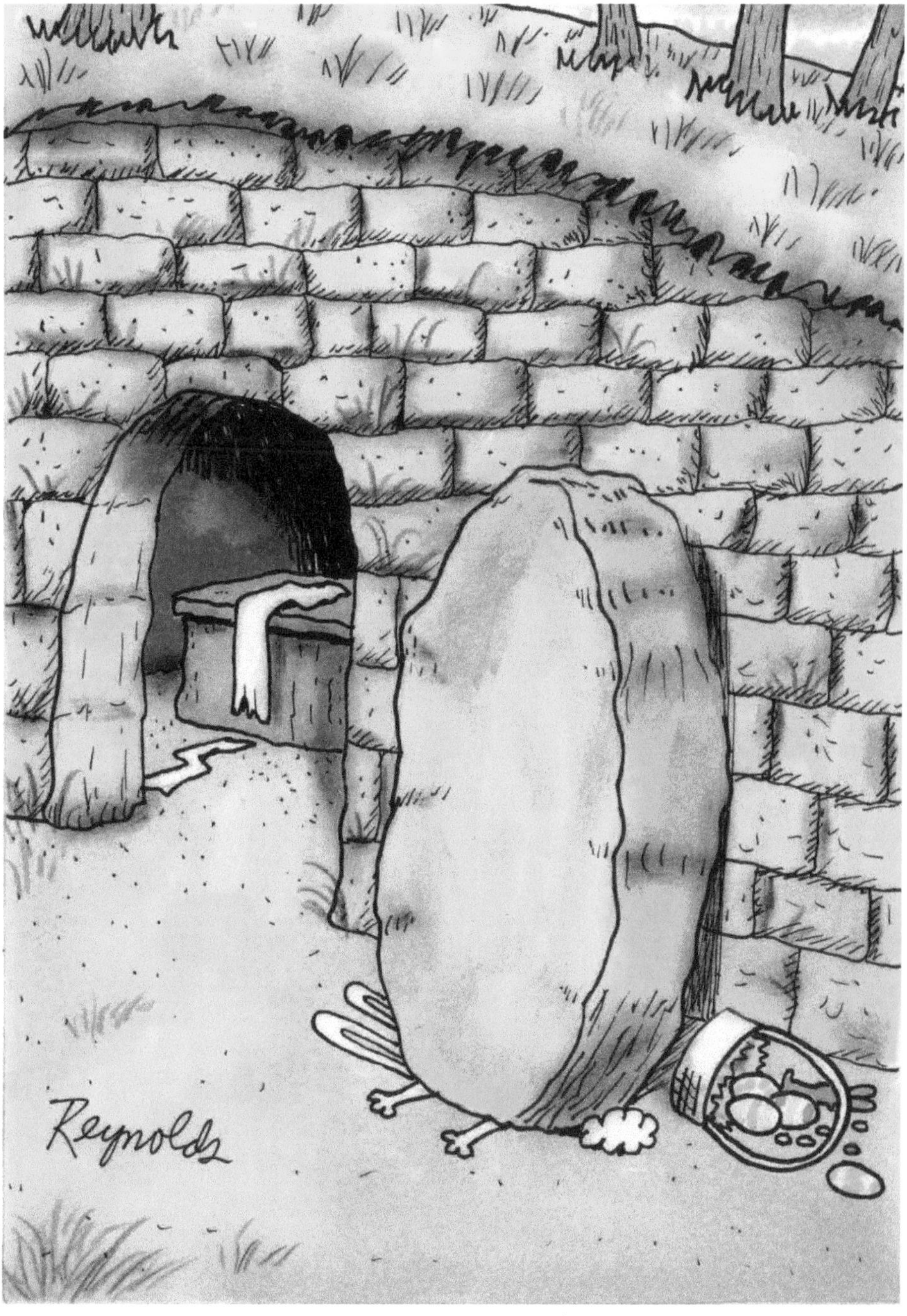
Reynolds

Life is God's way of speaking. Prayer is our way of understanding.

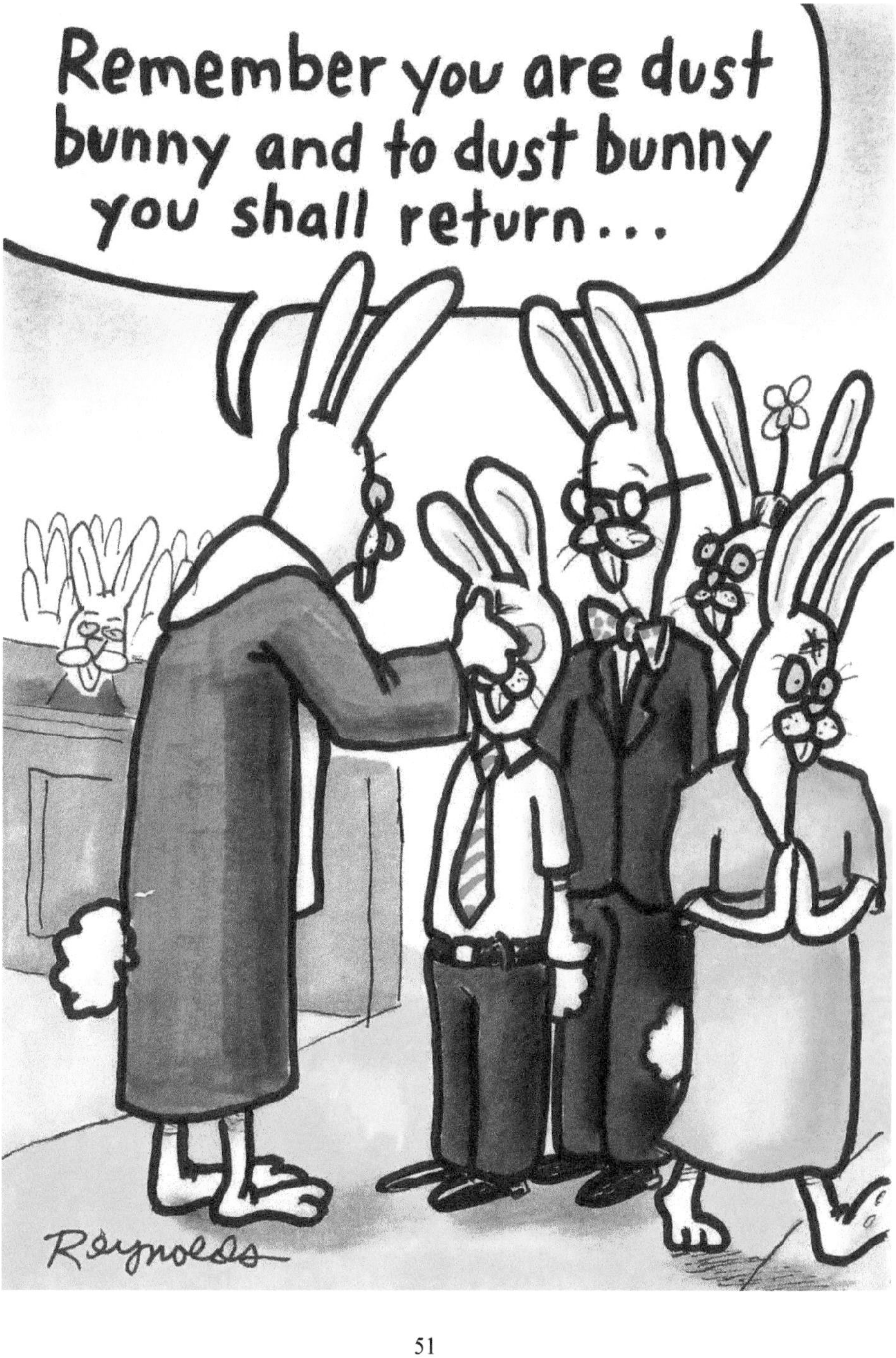
Remember you are dust bunny and to dust bunny you shall return...
Reynolds

Christians shouldn't give others a piece of their mind. They should give others peace of mind.

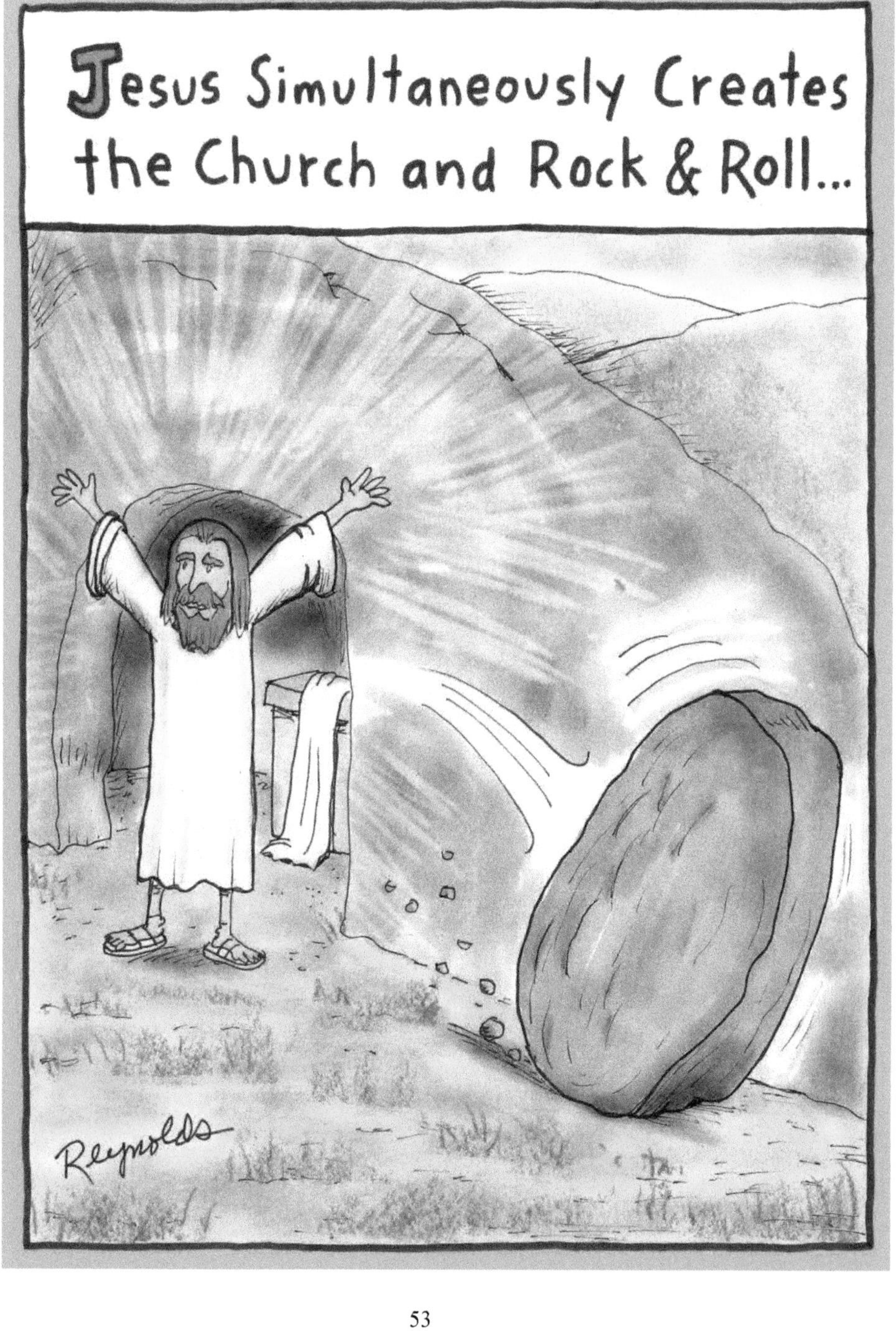
Jesus Simultaneously Creates the Church and Rock & Roll...
Reynolds

Jesus is the Word.
We should be the paper.

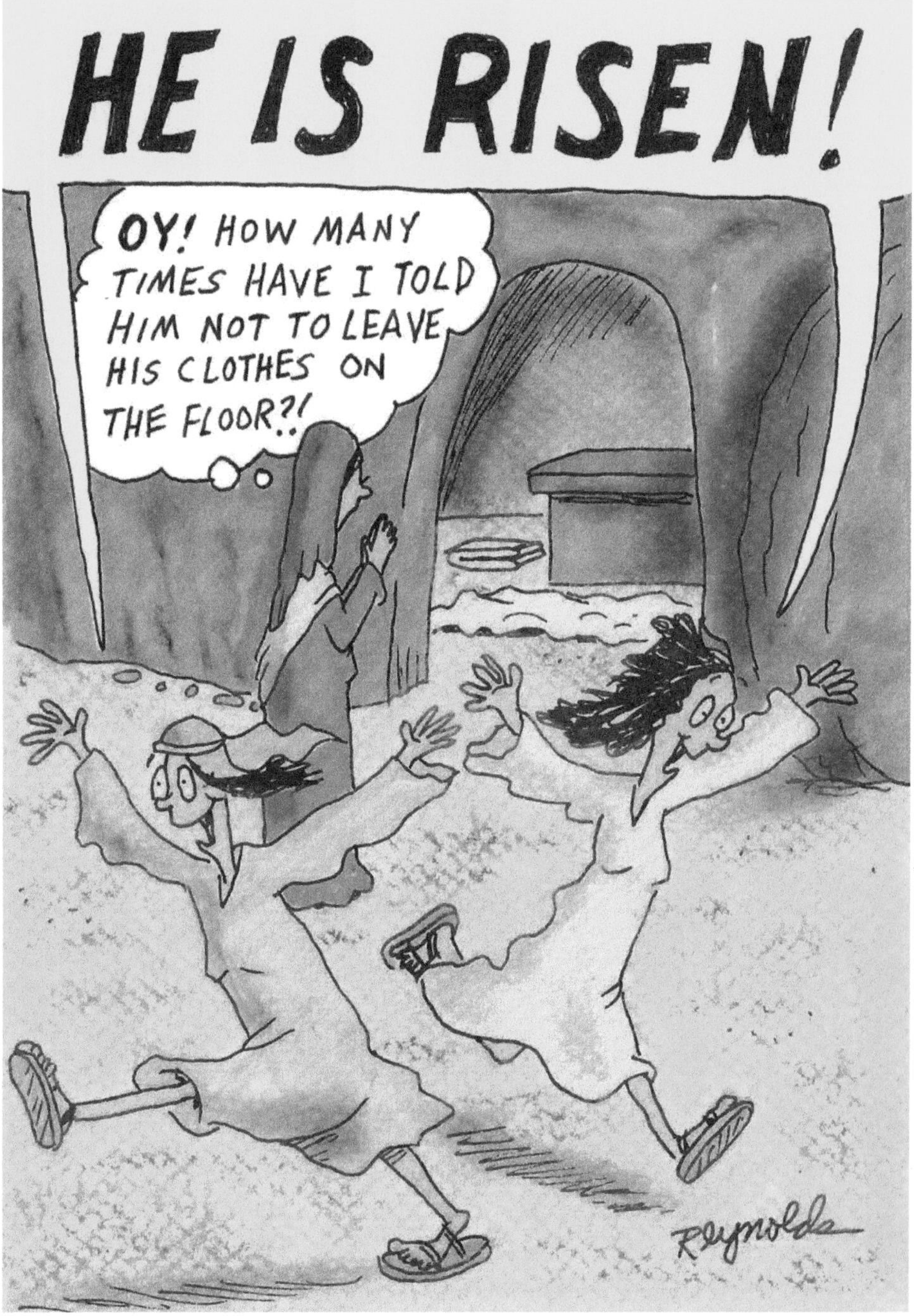
HE IS RISEN!
OY! HOW MANY TIMES HAVE I TOLD HIM NOT TO LEAVE HIS CLOTHES ON THE FLOOR?!
Reynolds

Love means pouring
yourself out so the
Grace of God
can fill up the space
between our today and
tomorrow.

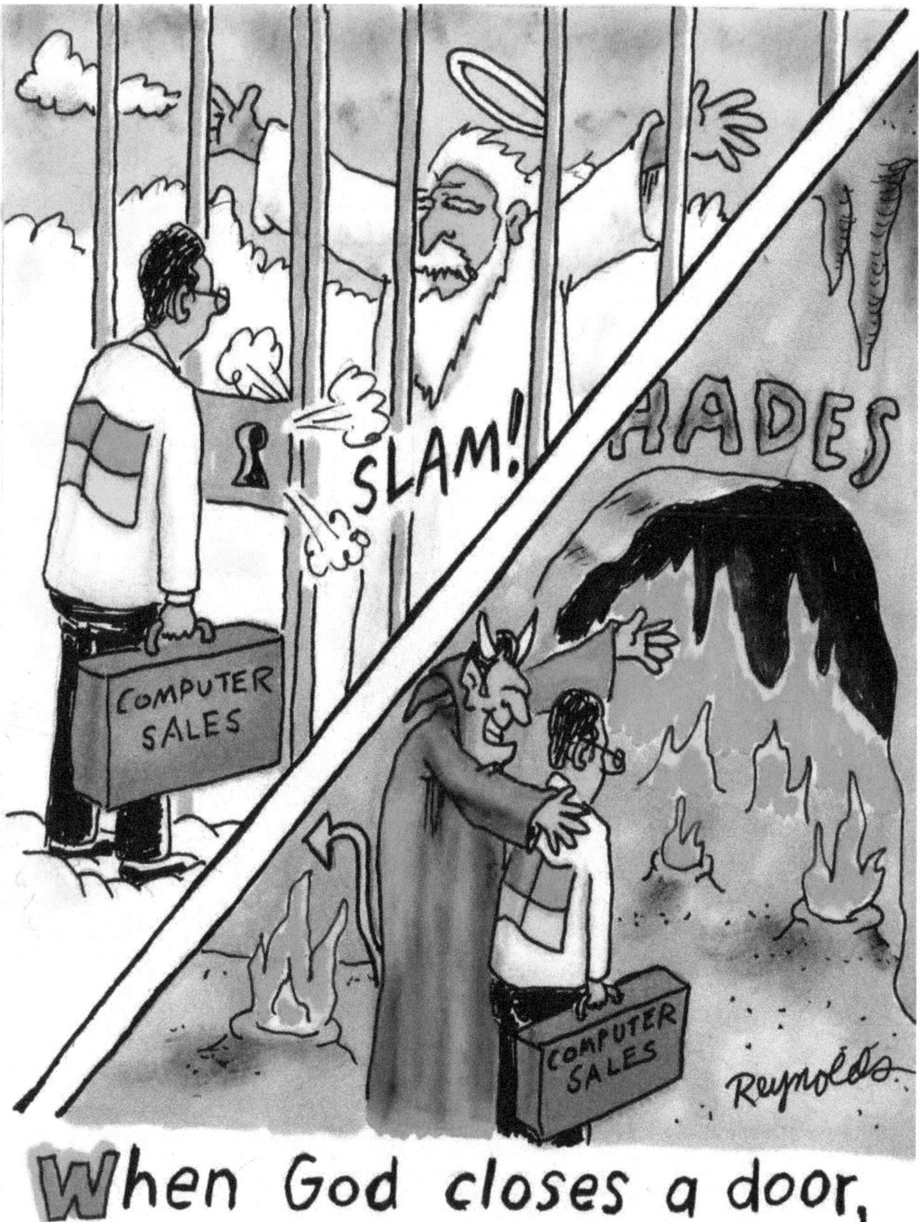
SLAM!
HADES
COMPUTER SALES
COMPUTER SALES
Reynolds

When God closes a door, somewhere He opens Windows.

Advice for the future: If you're standing in front of God and He asks if you've read His book, don't say, "No, I was waiting for the movie to come out."

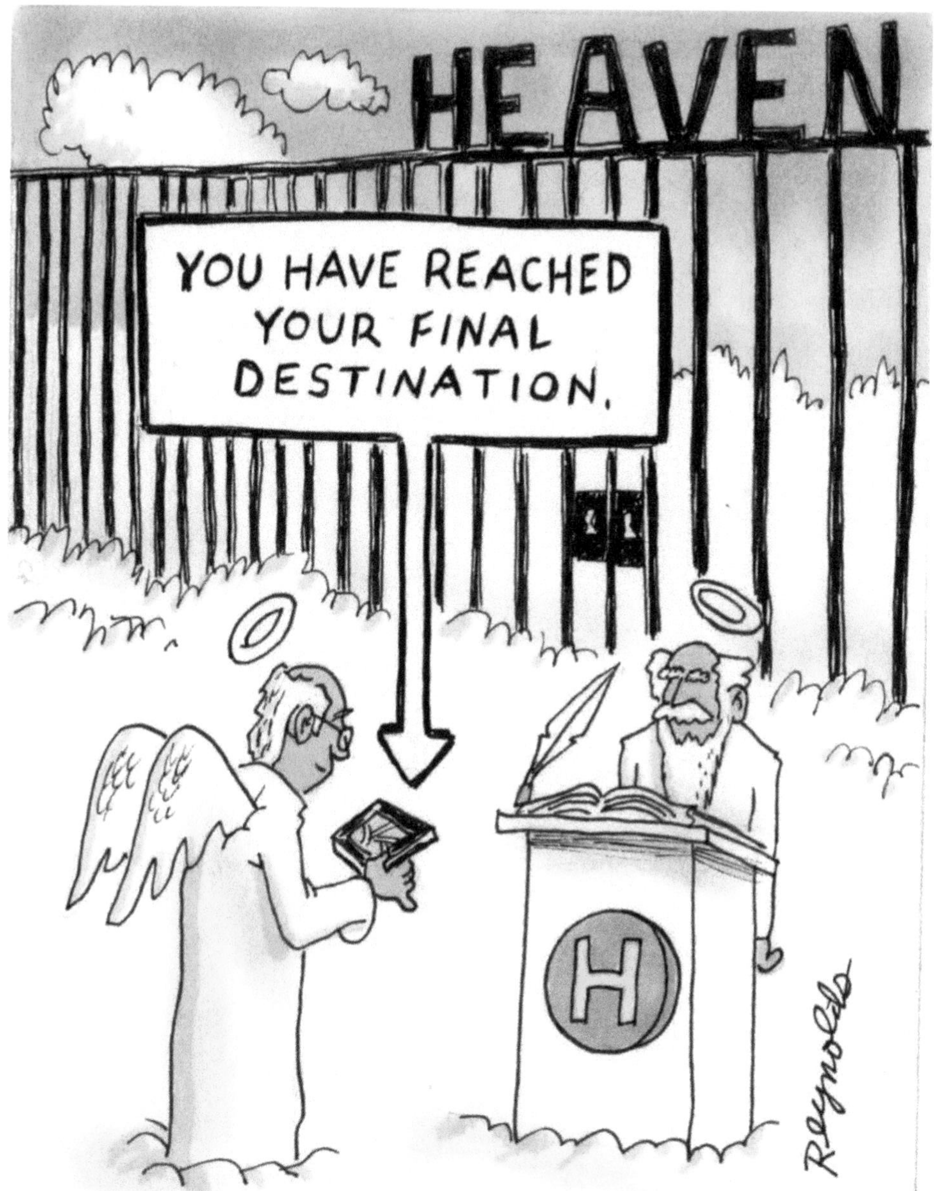
HEAVEN
YOU HAVE REACHED YOUR FINAL DESTINATION.
H
Reynolds

God Positioning System (GPS)

Heaven is such a hard concept to understand because it is always over our head.

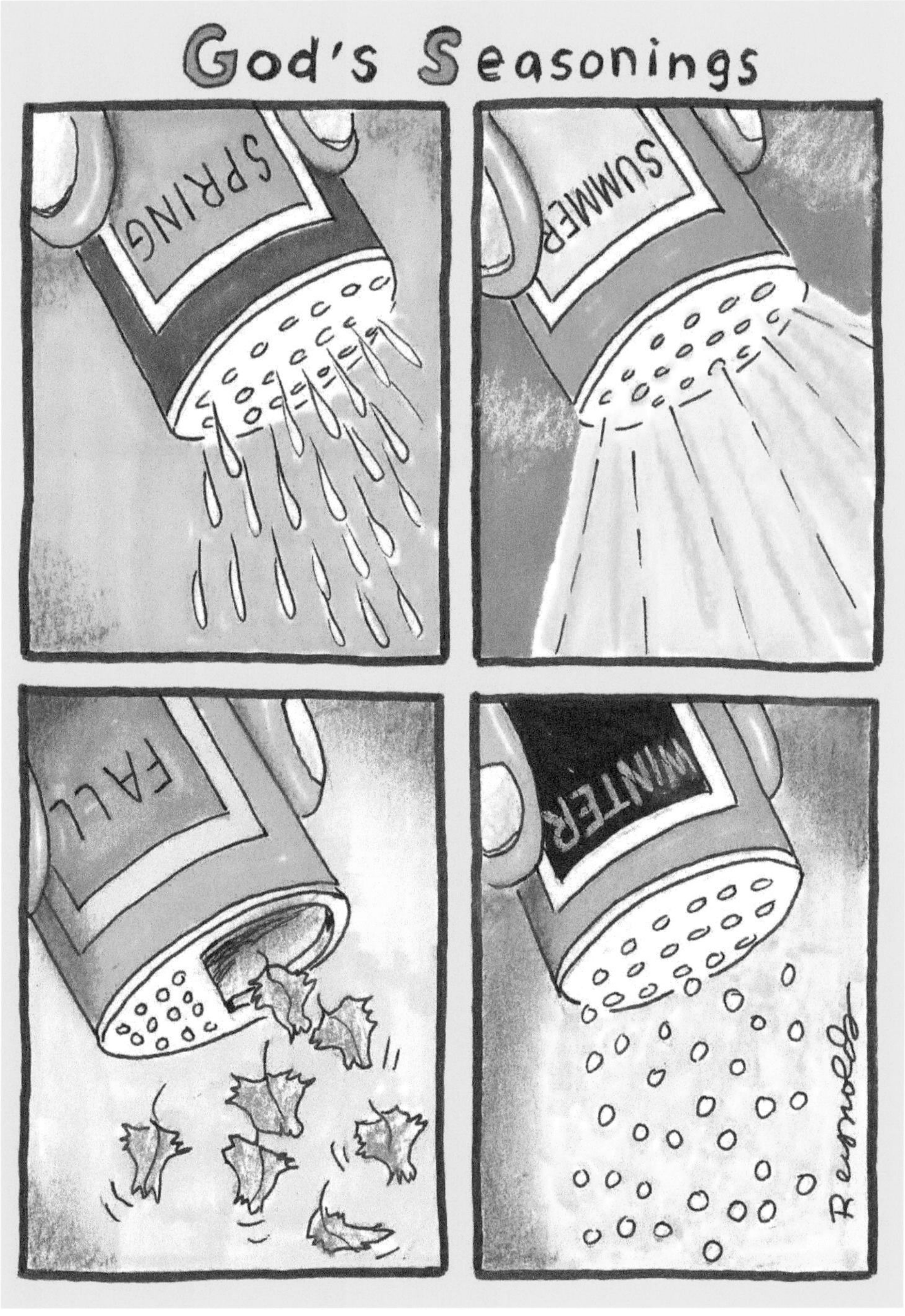
God's Seasonings
SPRING
SUMMER
FALL
WINTER
Reynolds

Things Jesus never said...
"I'm spiritual, but I'm not religious." This is like saying, I'm a son or daughter, but I don't believe in being part of a family.

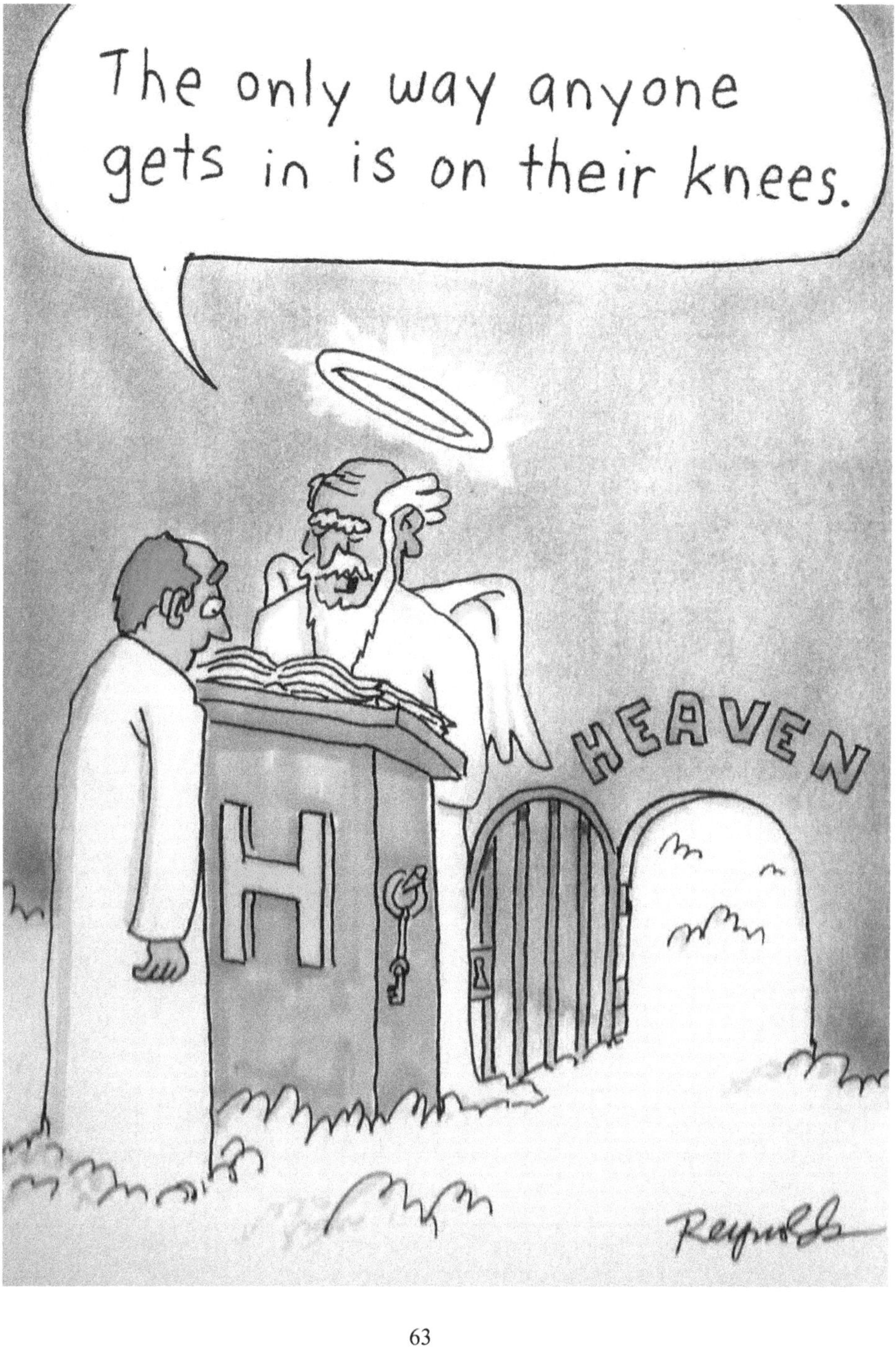
The only way anyone gets in is on their knees.
HEAVEN
H
Reynolds

The seeds of contemplation grow into the flowers of faith. The flowers of faith adorn the altar of charity.

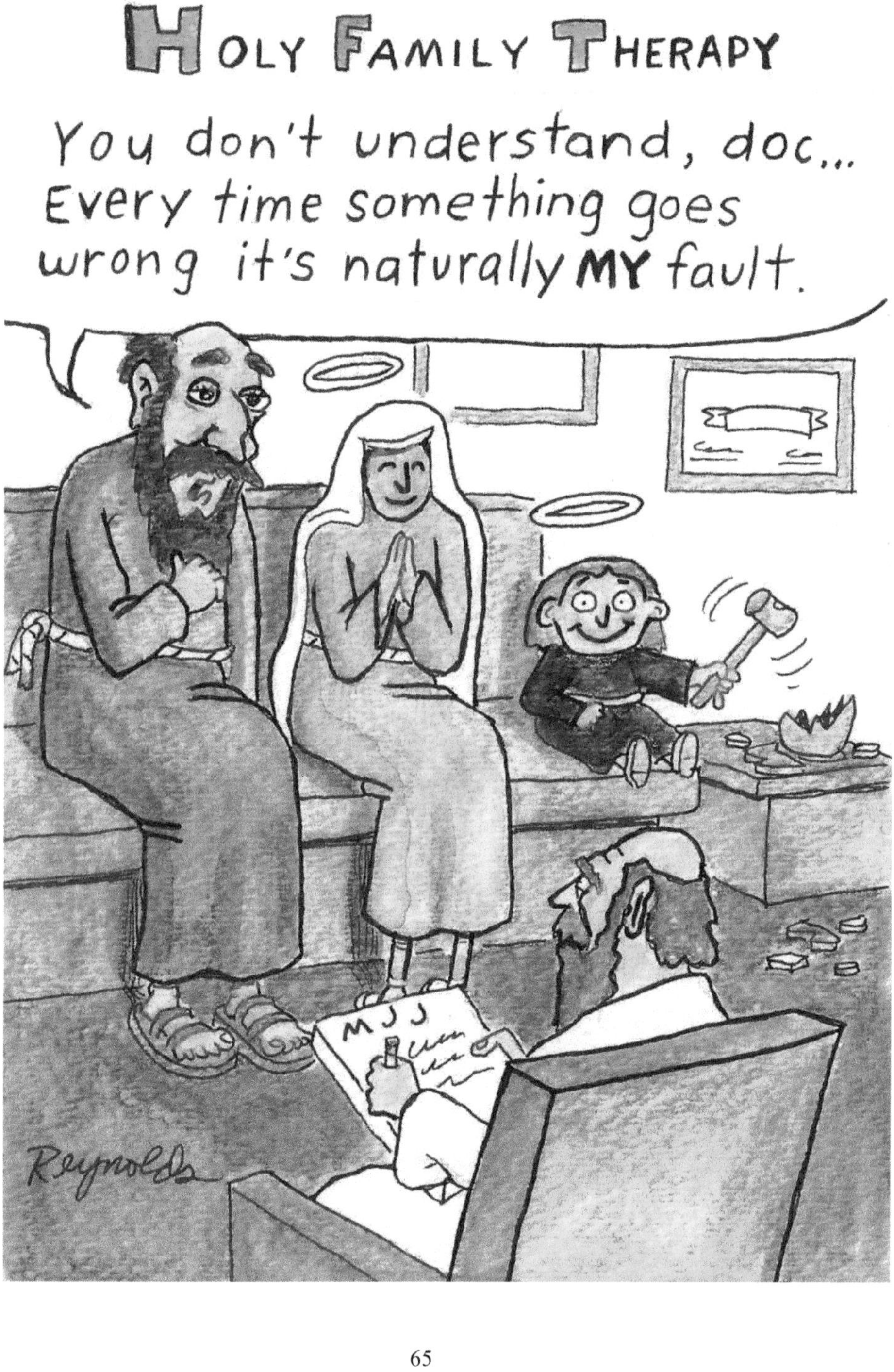
HOLY FAMILY THERAPY
You don't understand, doc... Every time something goes wrong it's naturally MY fault.
MJJ
Reynolds

The beginning of knowing
yourself is knowing exactly
when to "no" yourself.

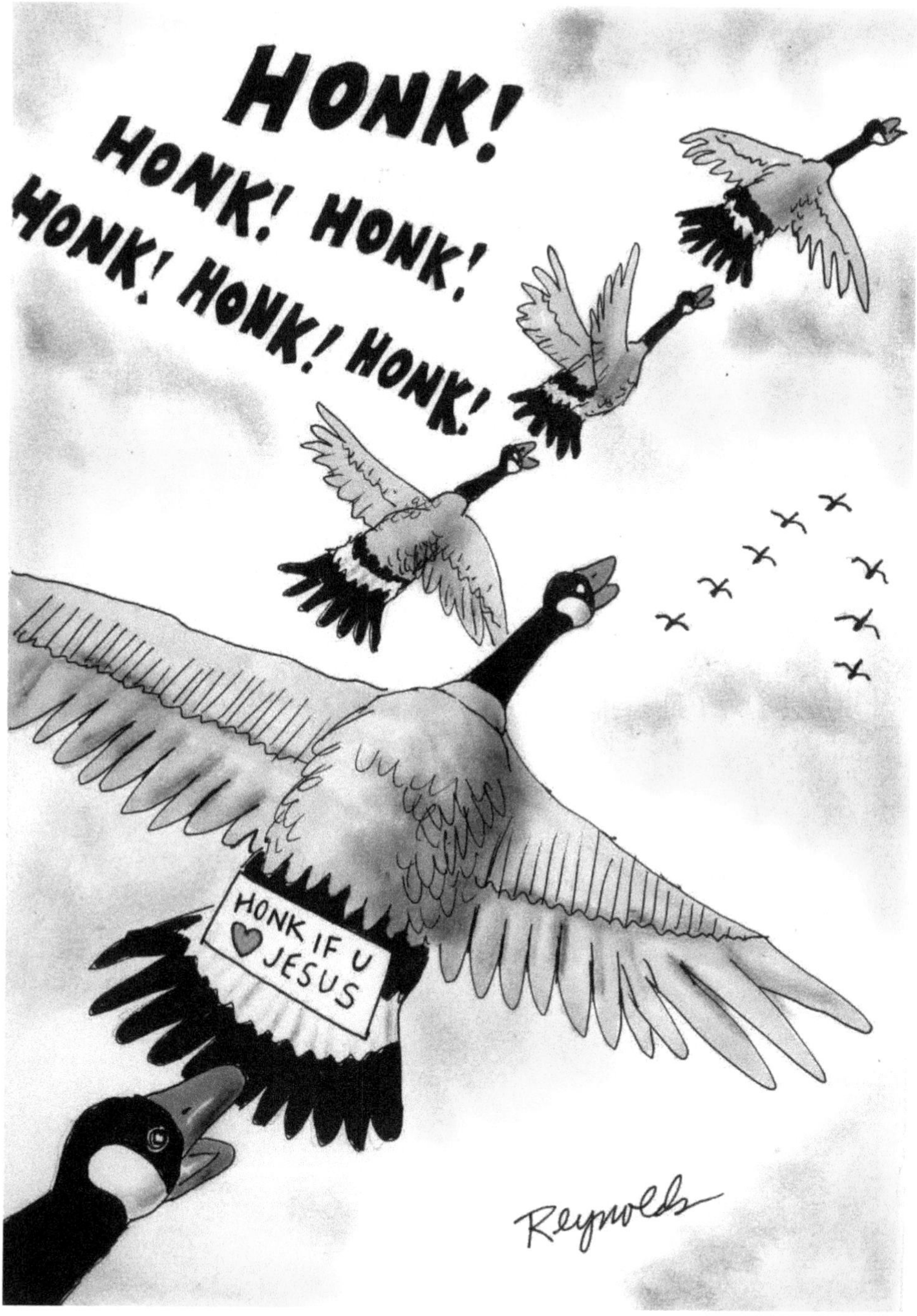
HONK!
HONK! HONK!
HONK! HONK! HONK!
HONK IF U ♥ JESUS
Reynolds

Joy is the **SON**rise
of the heart.

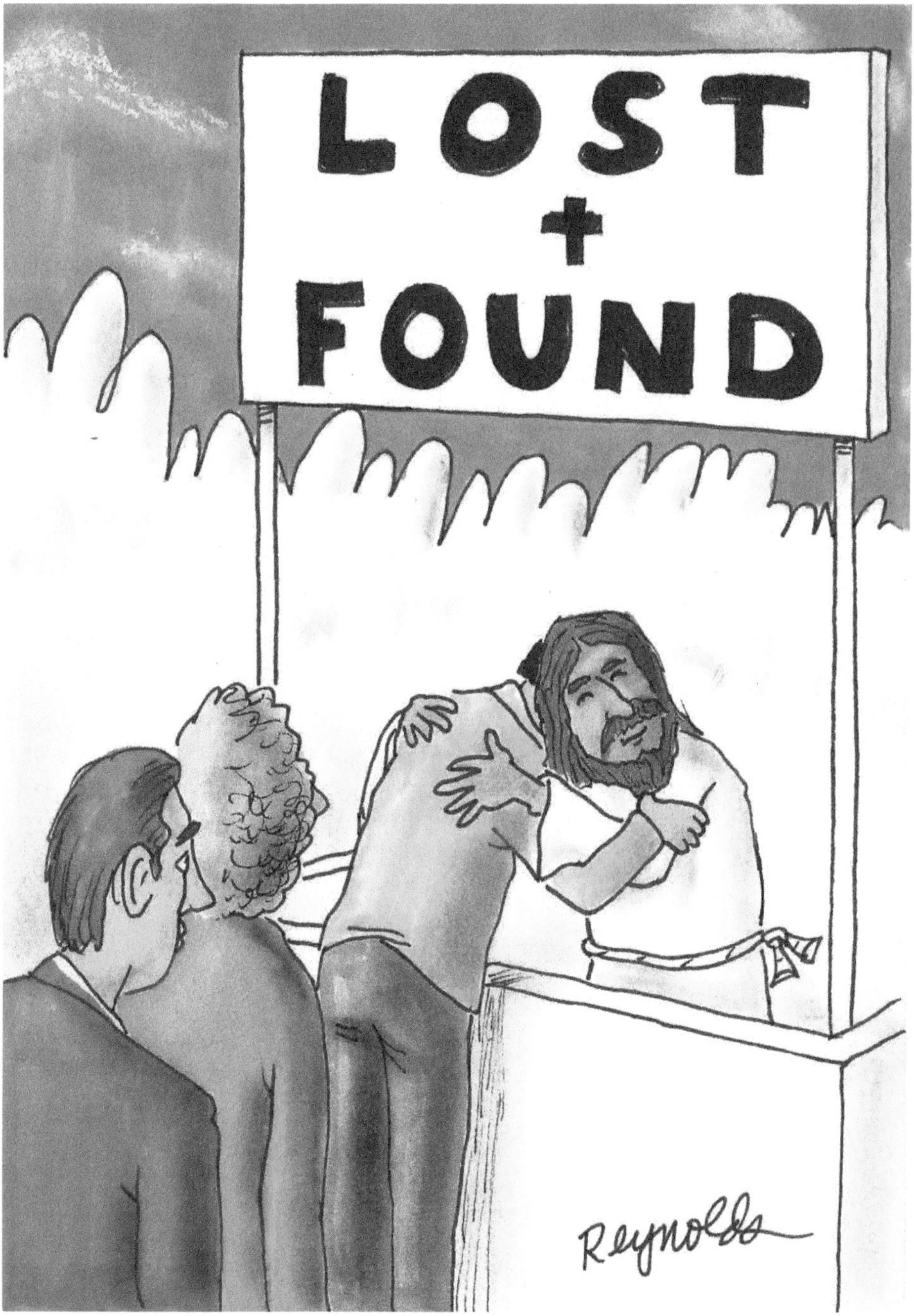
LOST
+
FOUND
Reynolds

Inside every "**pray**er there is a "ray" of **Son**shine.

JESUS WALKS ON WALKER

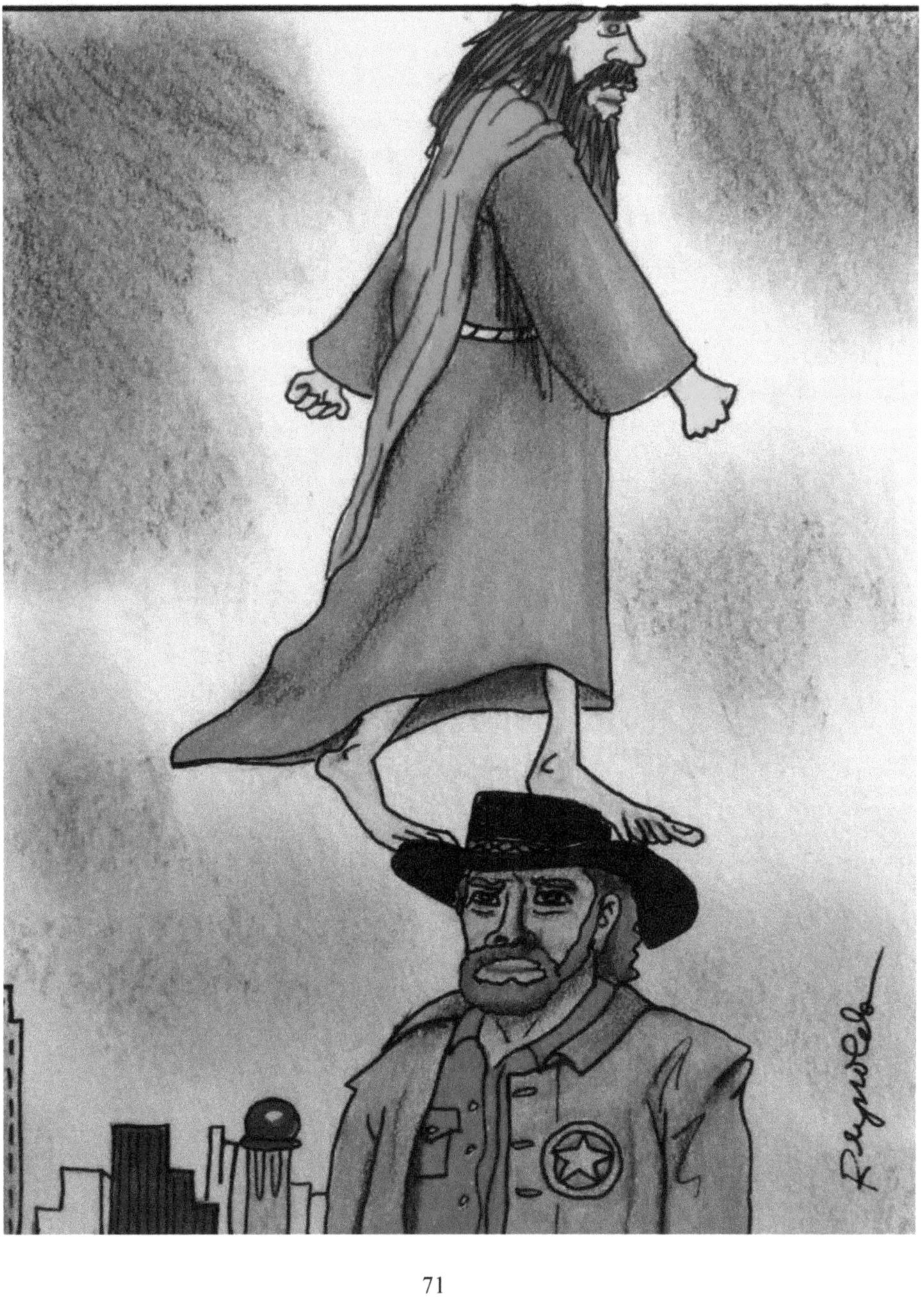

God never gives us more
than we can handle,
because He helps us handle
whatever we are given.

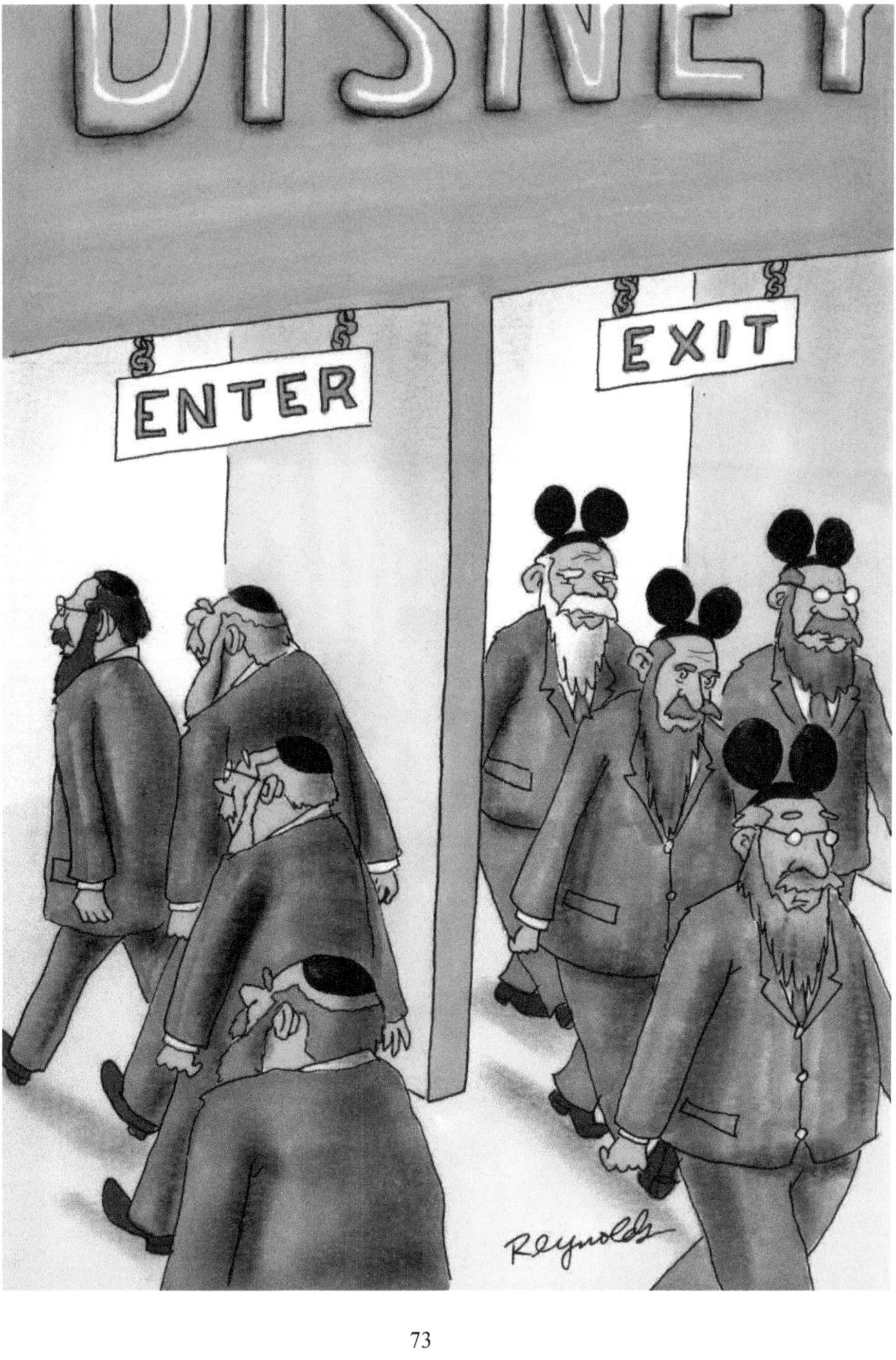
DISNEY
ENTER
EXIT
Reynolds

God made smiles so that they would point to Heaven.

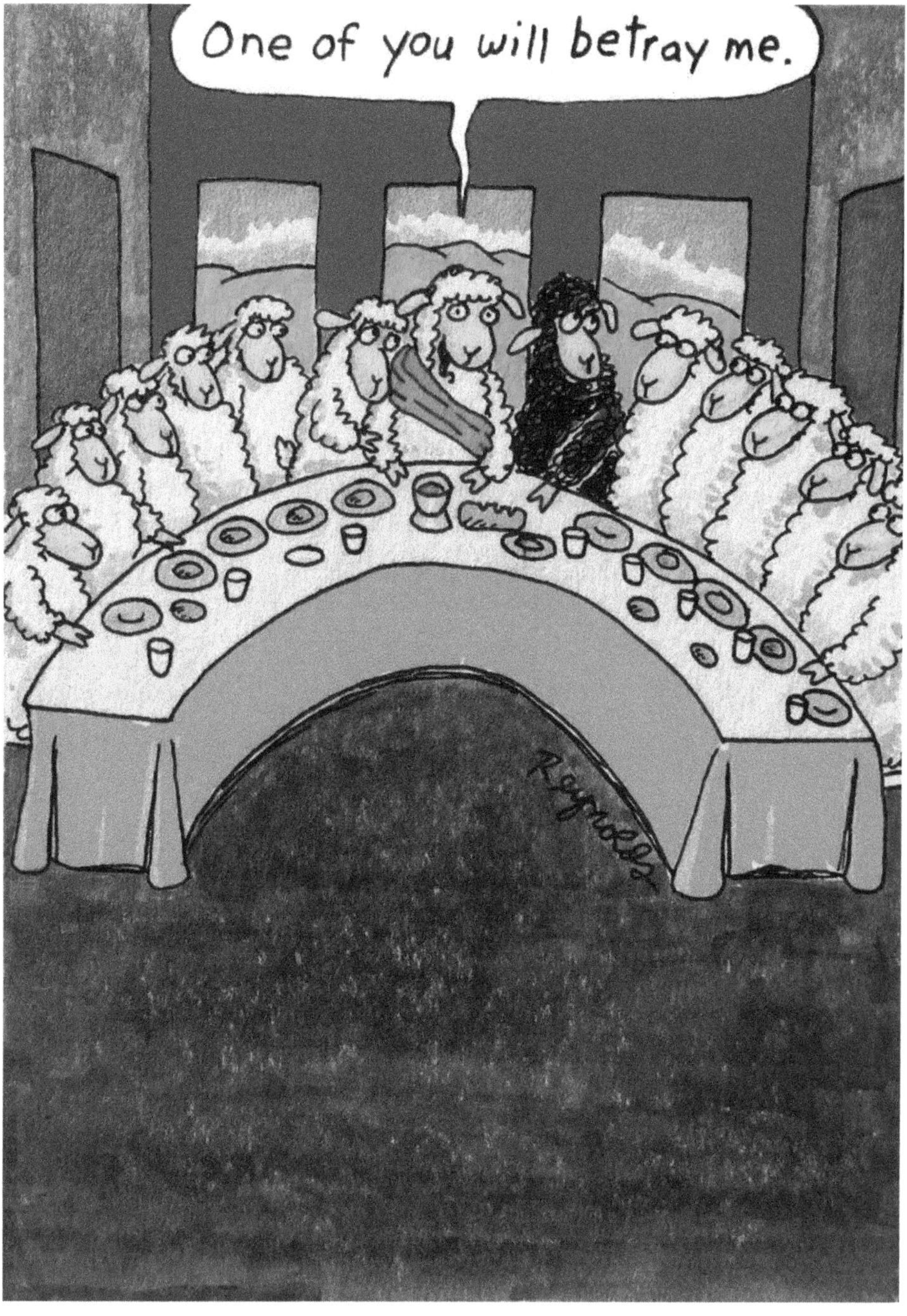
One of you will betray me.
Reynolds

God holds us in the palm of His Hand, and if we look closely at ourselves we can see God's fingerprints all over us.

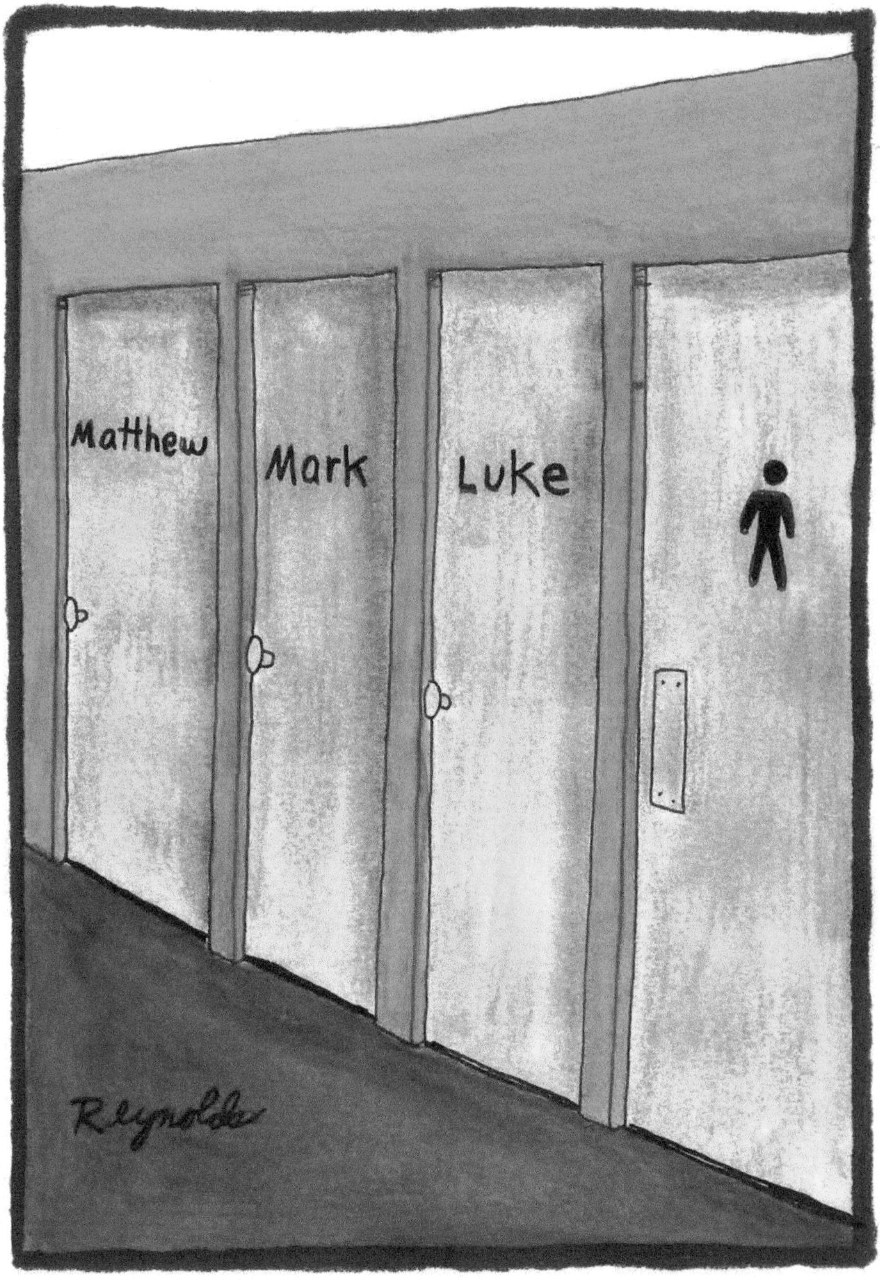
Matthew
Mark
Luke
Reynolds

Holy Laughter...going from "Ha-Ha" to "A-ha" to Amen".

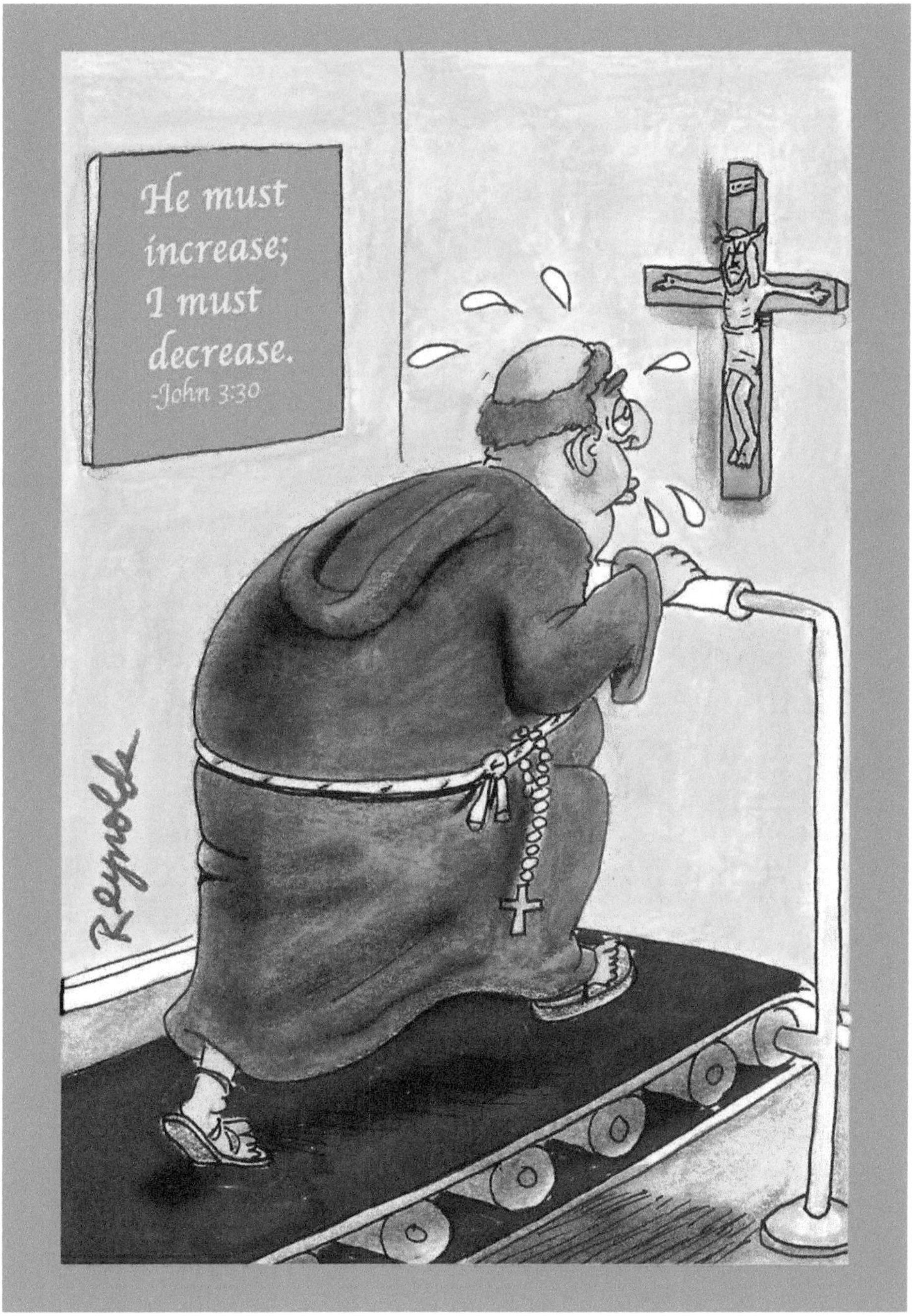
He must
increase;
I must
decrease.
-John 3:30
Reynolds

Life is like a box of chocolates. You always know what you're going to get...FAT!

Moses, after forty years in the desserts...

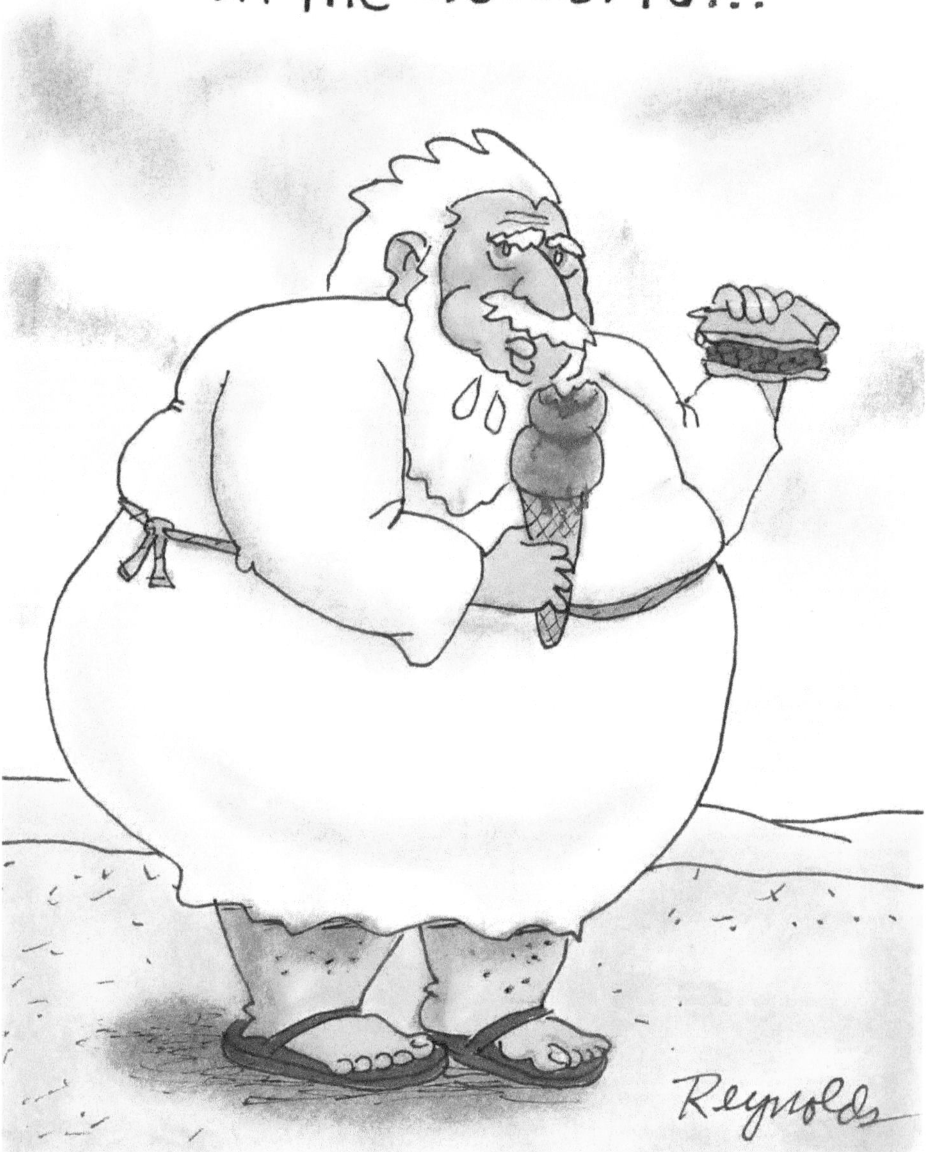
Reynolds

The best laughter hits you right in the belly. That's why the middle of laughter is "ugh!"

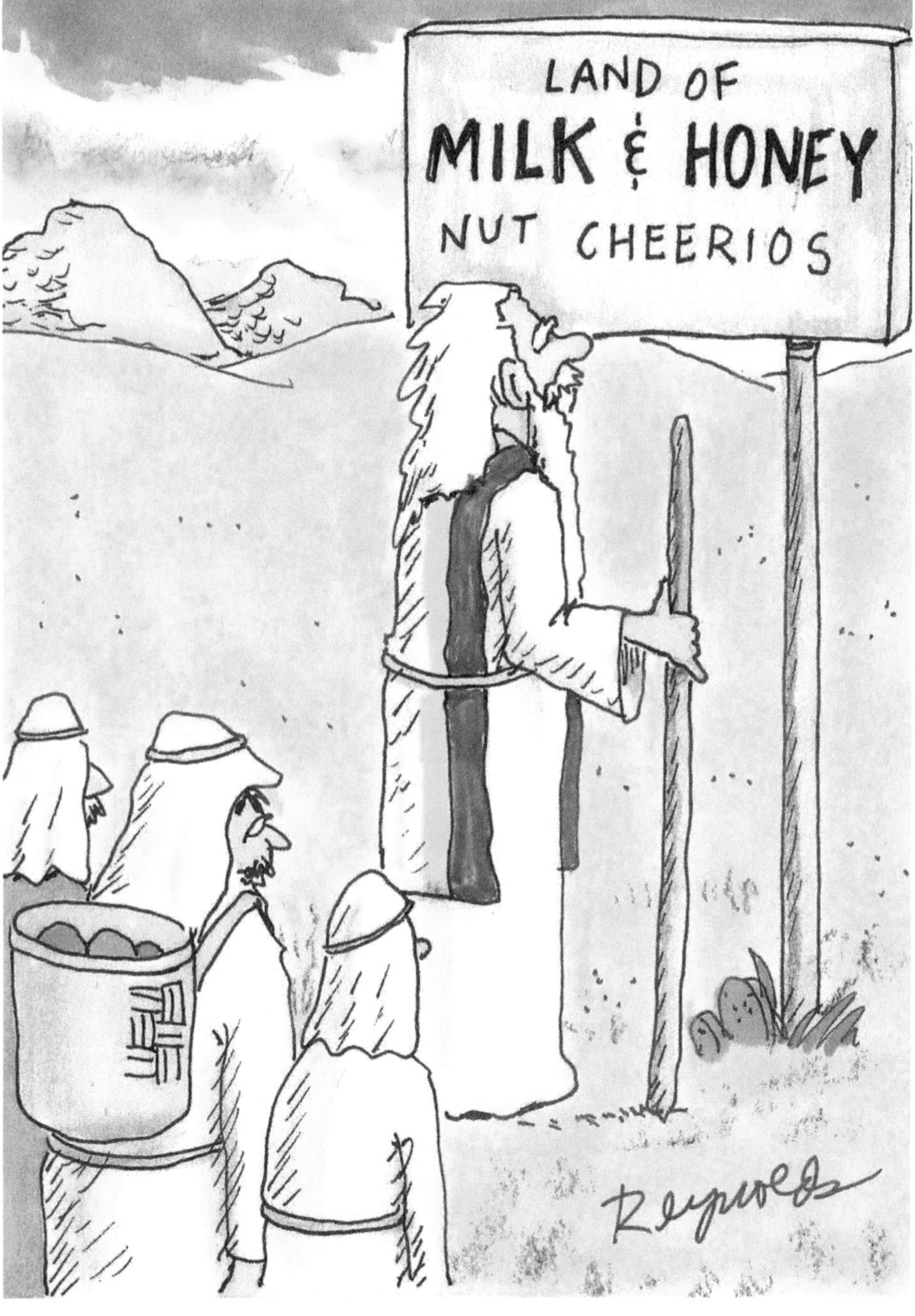
LAND OF
MILK & HONEY
NUT CHEERIOS
Reynolds

If you possess the ability to laugh so hard you cry as well as cry so hard you laugh, then your body and spirit are well balanced.

MOSES LOST IN THE DESERT...YEAR 40

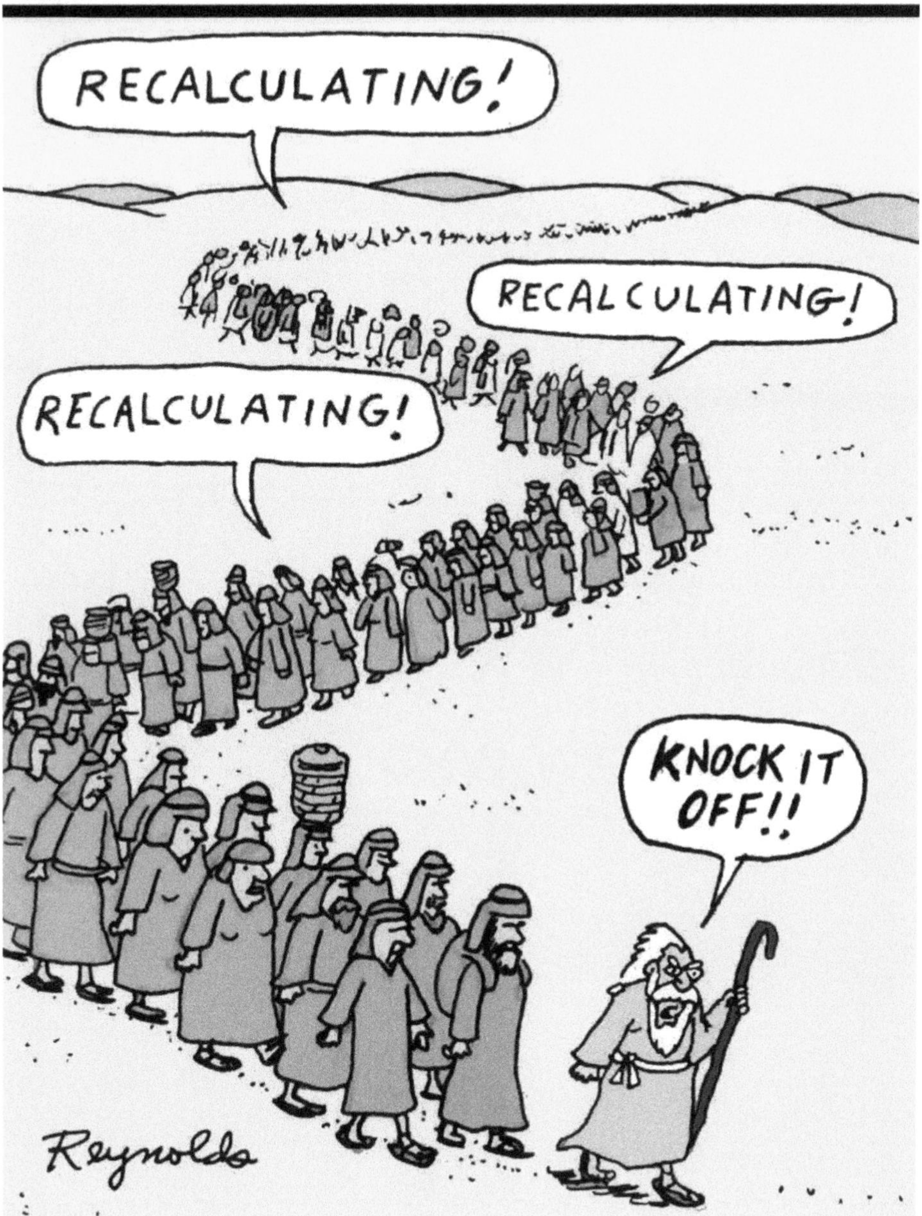
RECALCULATING!
RECALCULATING!
RECALCULATING!
KNOCK IT OFF!!
Reynolds

If we spent as much time wondering who God is as we spend wondering who we are, we would know exactly who we are.

MOSES WATERS HIS DAISIES...

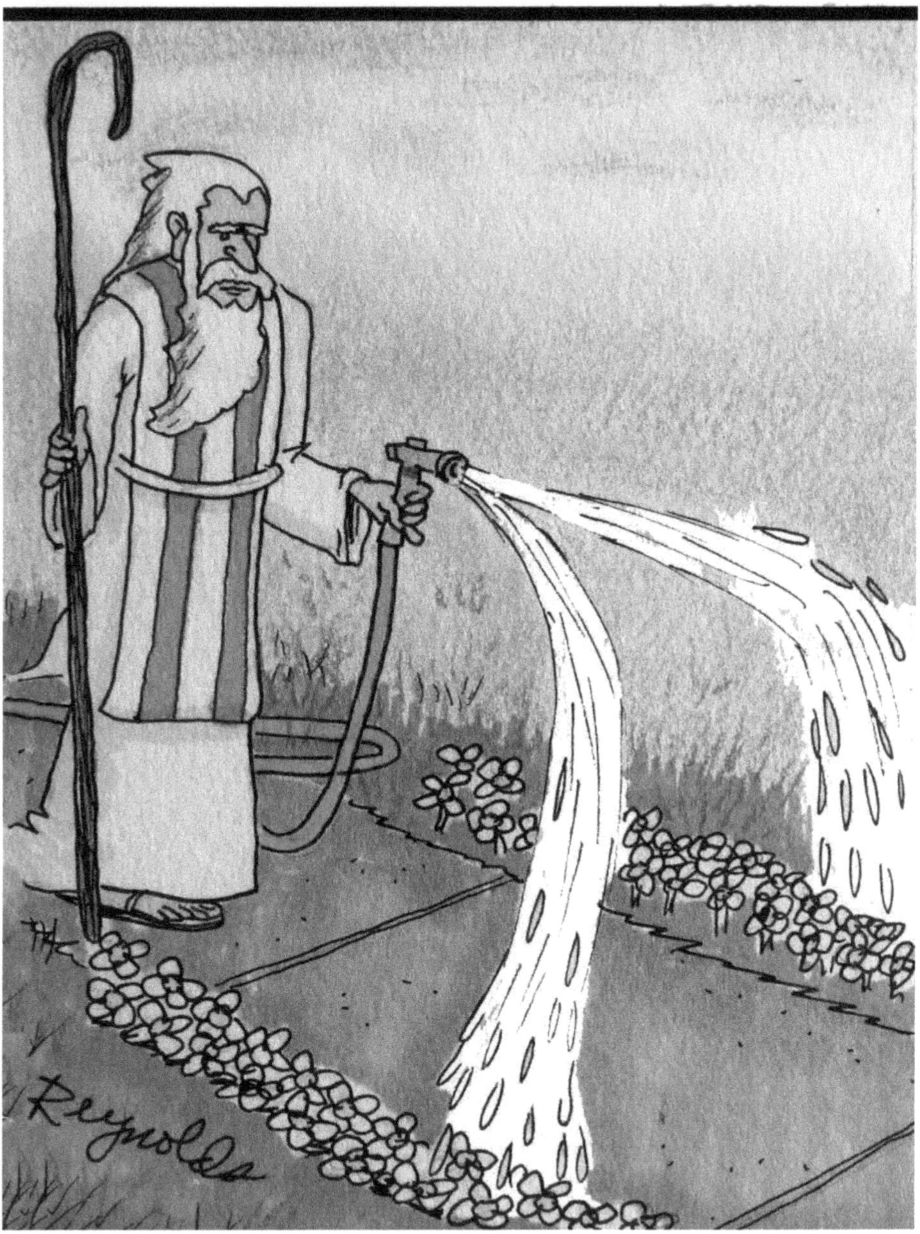
Reynolds

When we say, "I'd like things to be different", do we include ourselves in those "things" or do we just mean everything else in the world?

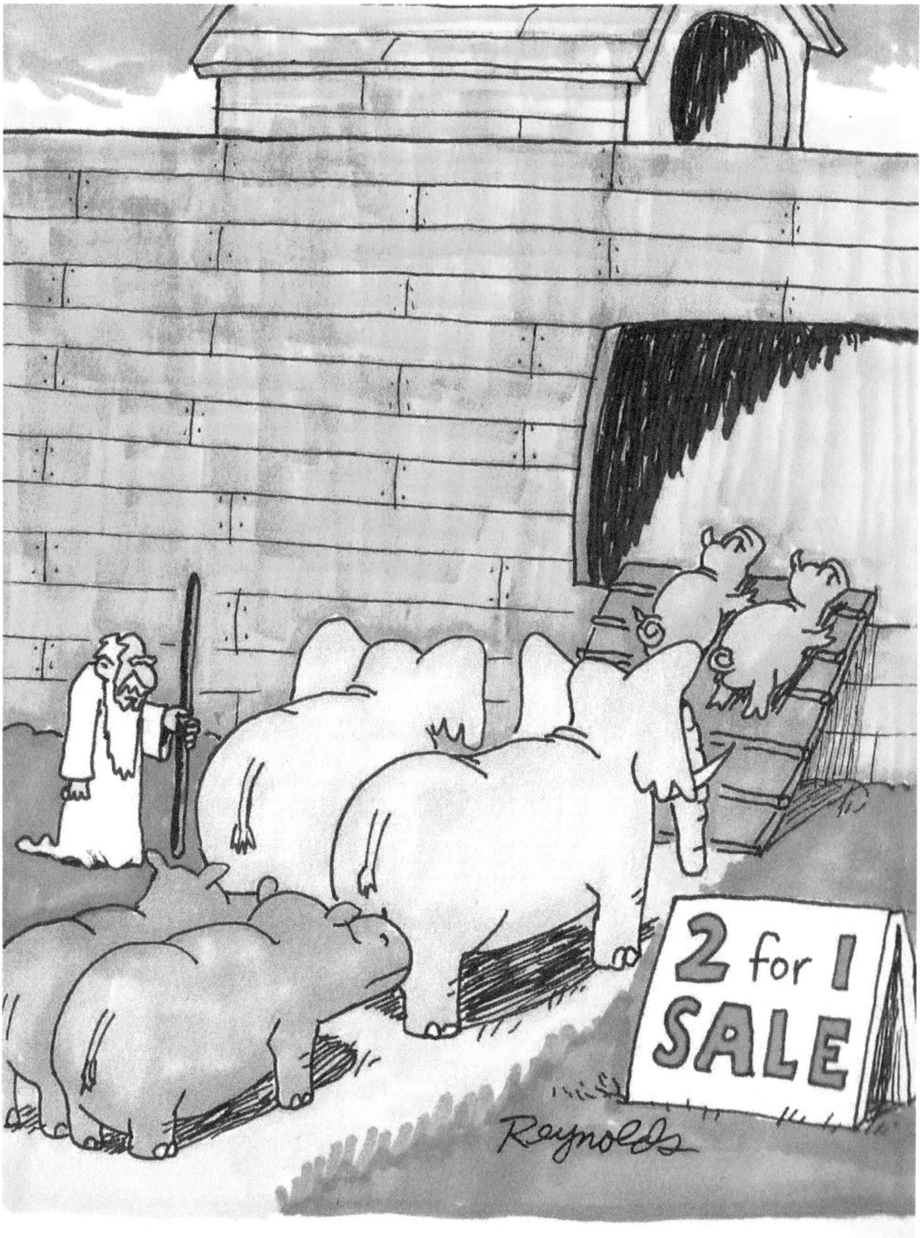
2 for 1
SALE
Reynolds

How Noah did it.

Marriage is saying "I do" to your spouse just as God says, "I AM" to His Church.

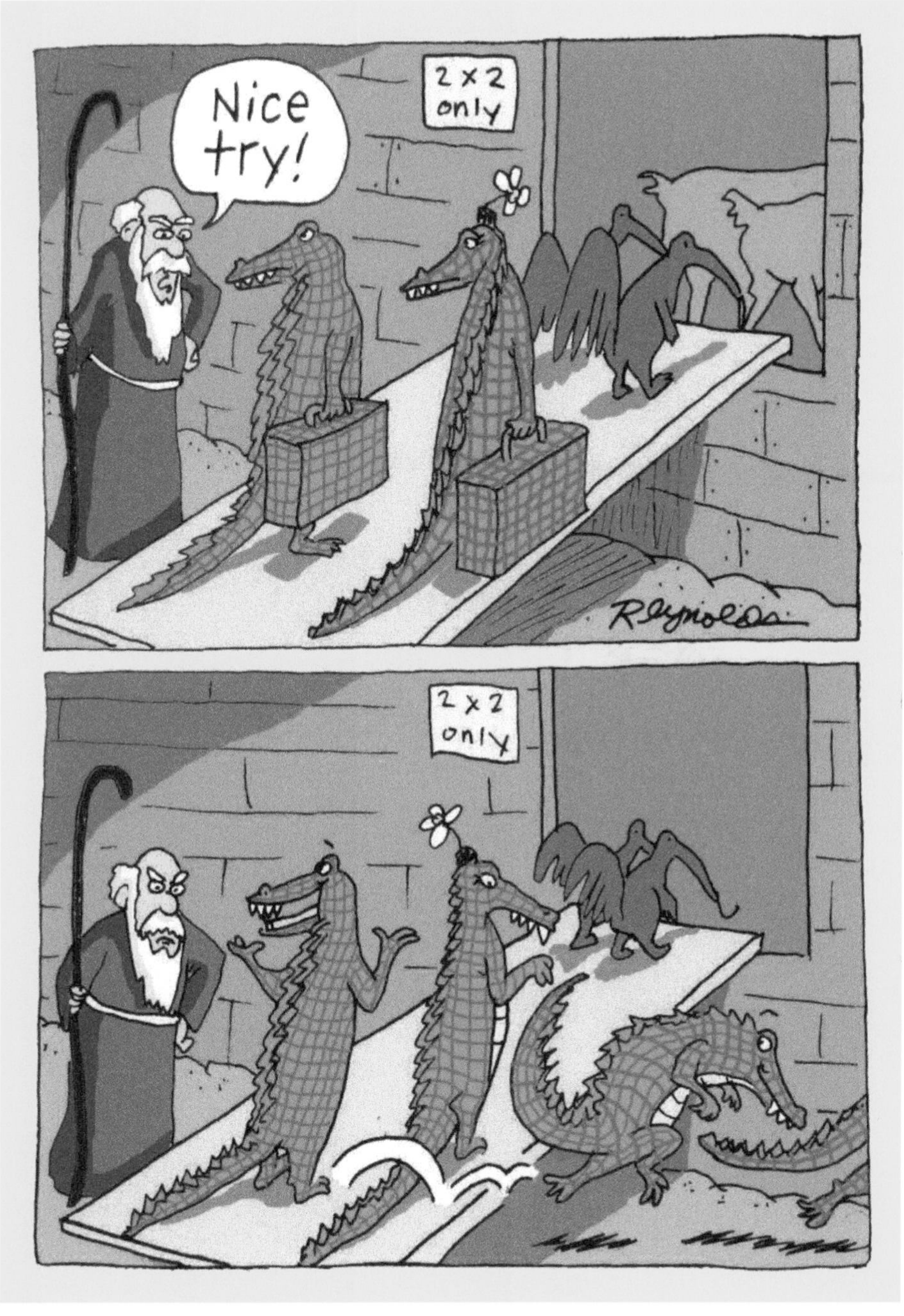
2 x 2
only
Nice
try!
RReynolds
2 x 2
only

The devil speaks to us in fear. God speaks to us in prayer.

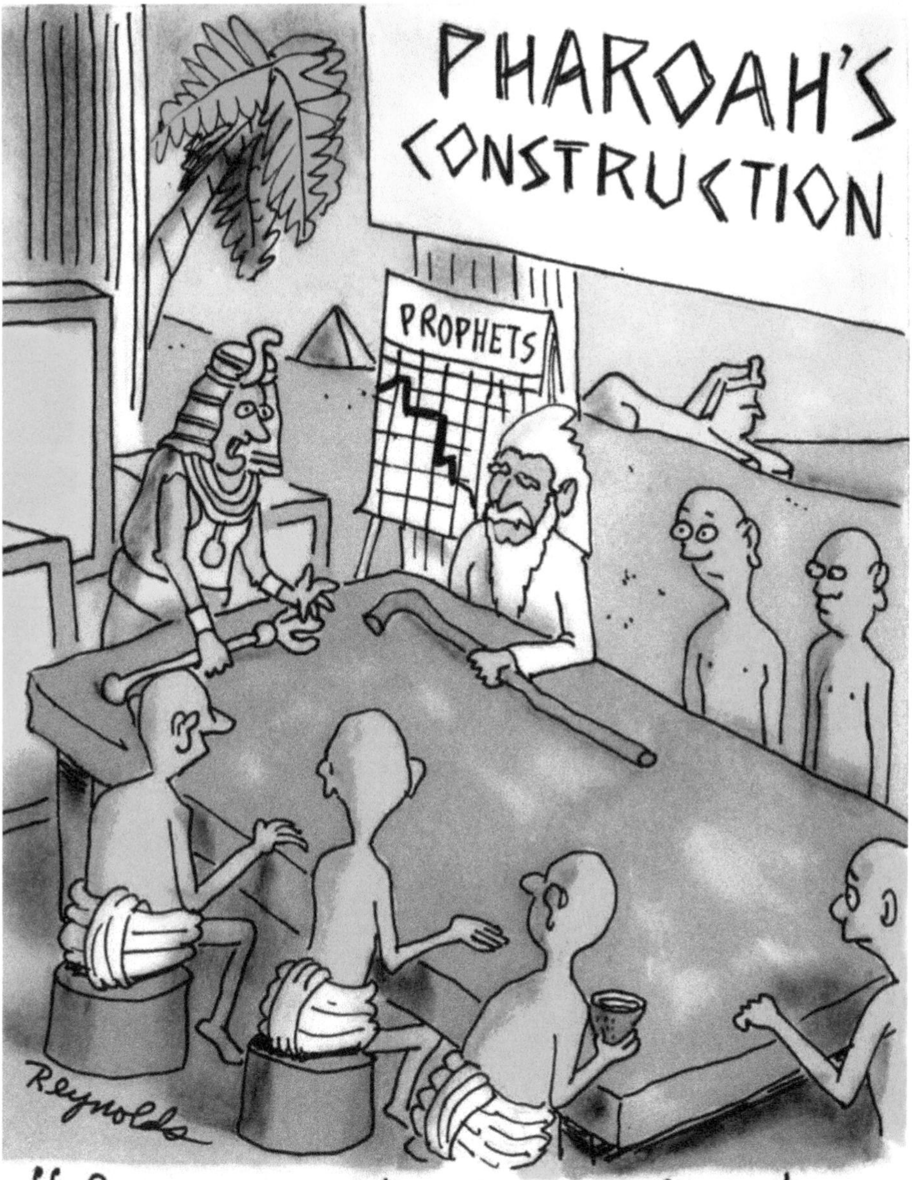
PHAROAH'S
CONSTRUCTION
PROPHETS
Reynolds

"Sorry, people, I'm going to have to let you go..."

Tears of Joy are like raindrops from Heaven that water the flowers of faith.

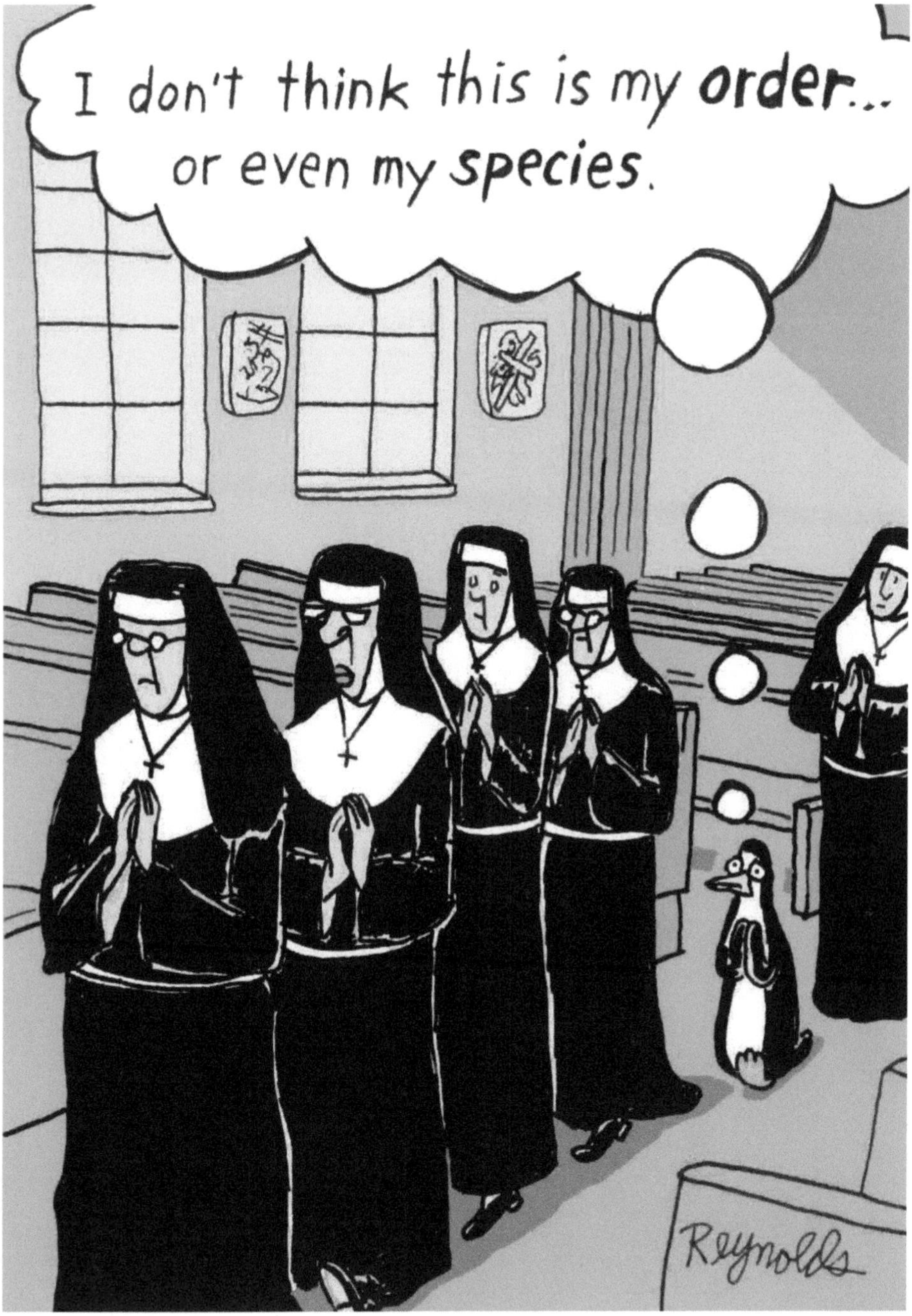
I don't think this is my order...
or even my species.
Reynolds

Mother Teresa, Teresa of Lisieux, and Teresa of Avila walked into the best bar in Heaven..."Bar Nun".

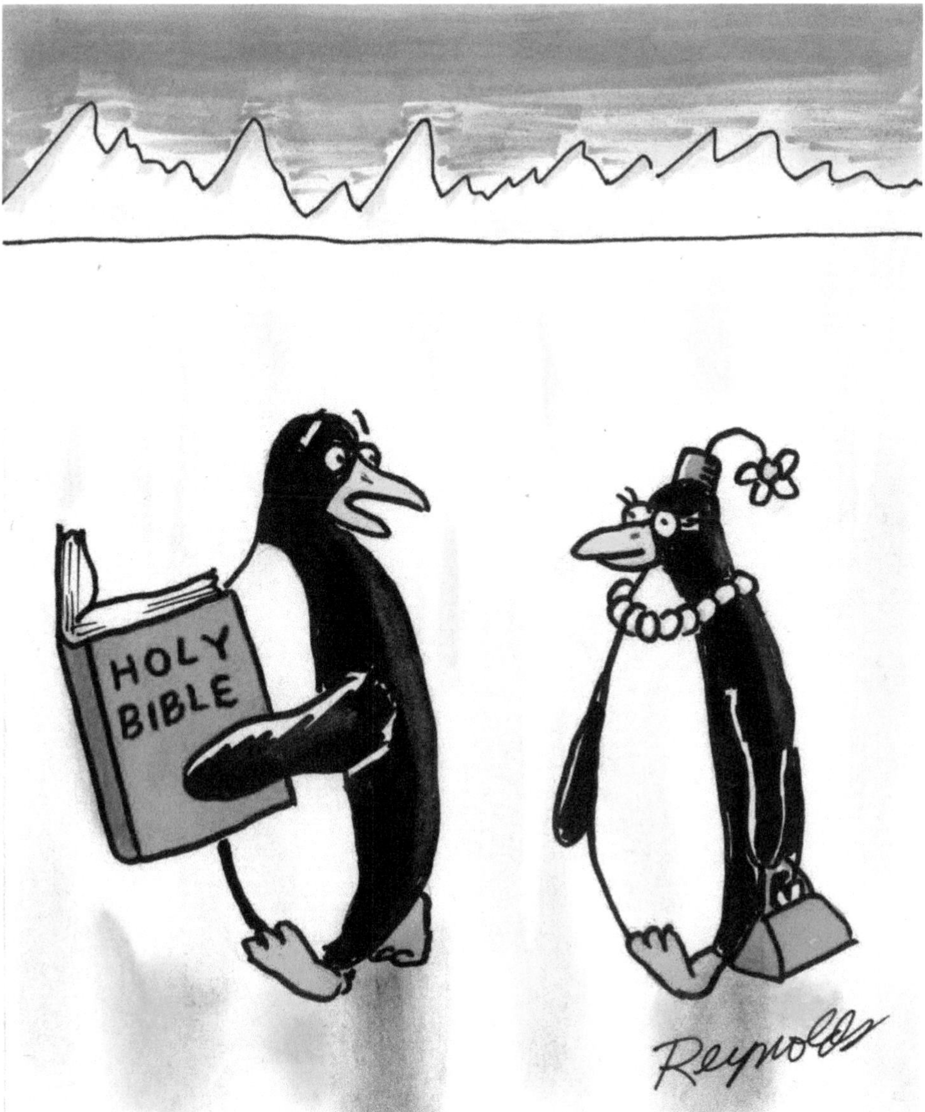
HOLY
BIBLE
Reynolds

"What am I missing here? We walk on water all the time."

A leap of faith should never include a jump to conclusions.

Peter, you will deny me THREE times...
I will never deny you, Lord.
Yes, you will.
No, I won't.
YES, you will.
No, I WON'T!
HEY!

There is no such thing as an original thought because God has always thought of it first.

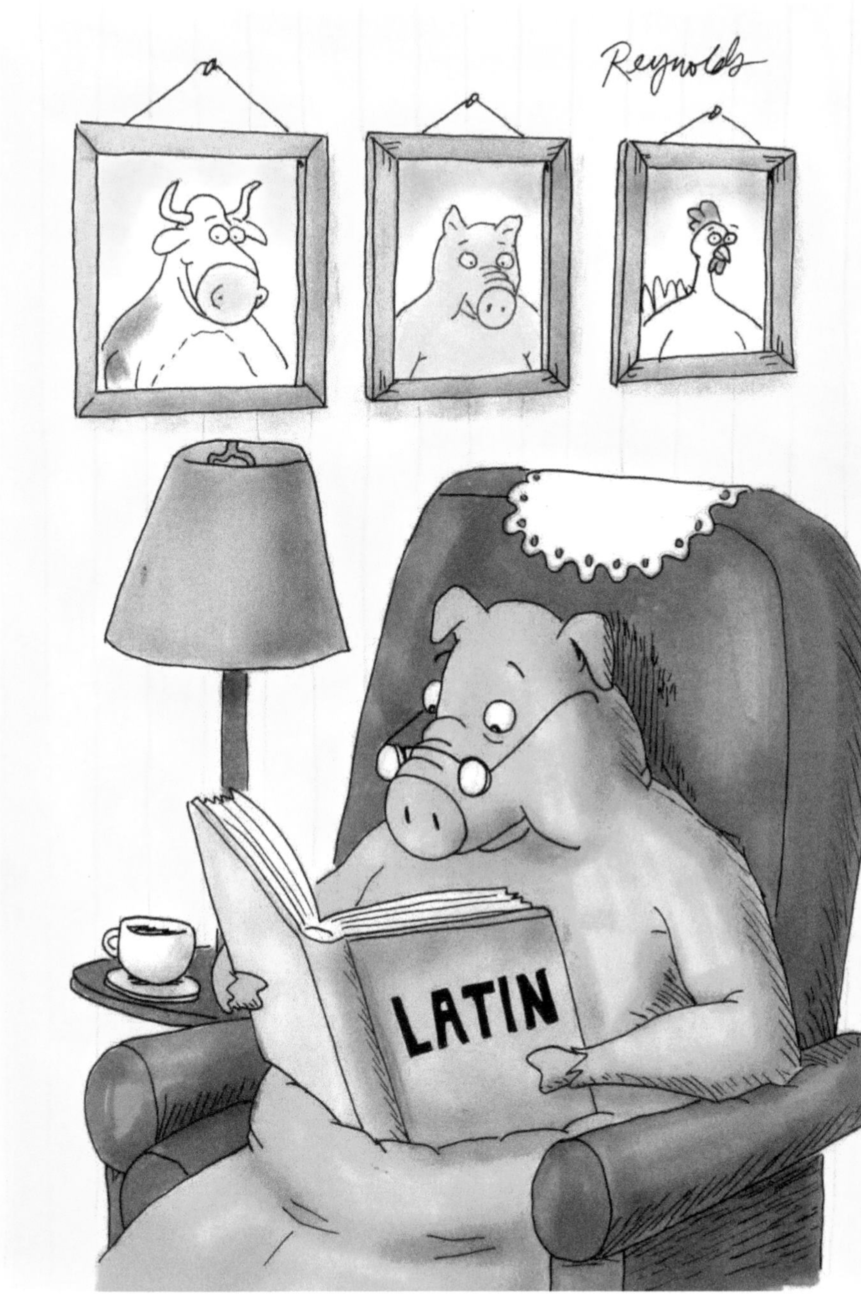
Reynolds
LATIN

Expecting to find yourself in a self-help book is like giving yourself a hug. You always end up full of yourself. Empty.

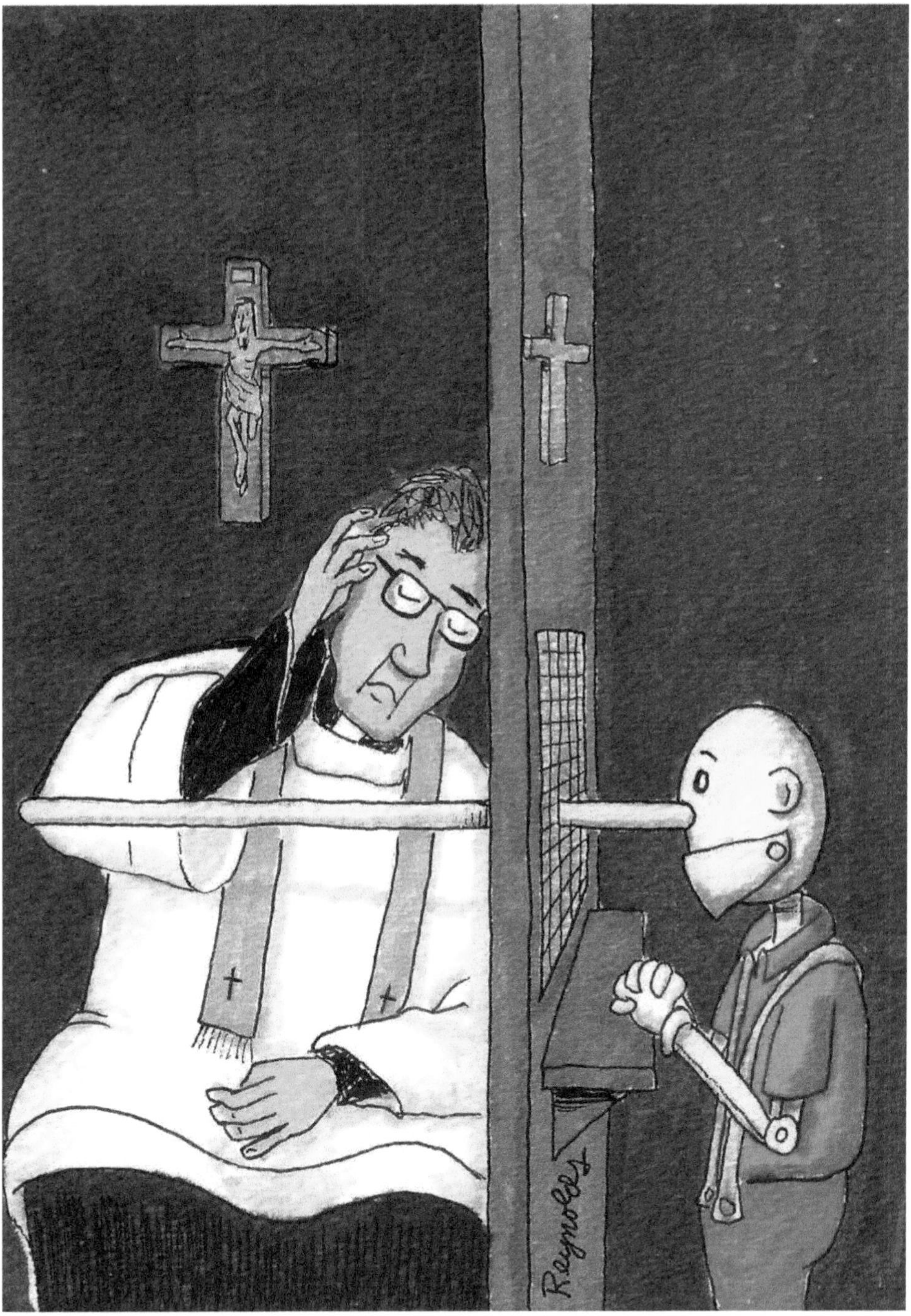
Reynolds

Focusing on others' sins and not your own is like breathing out without ever breathing in.

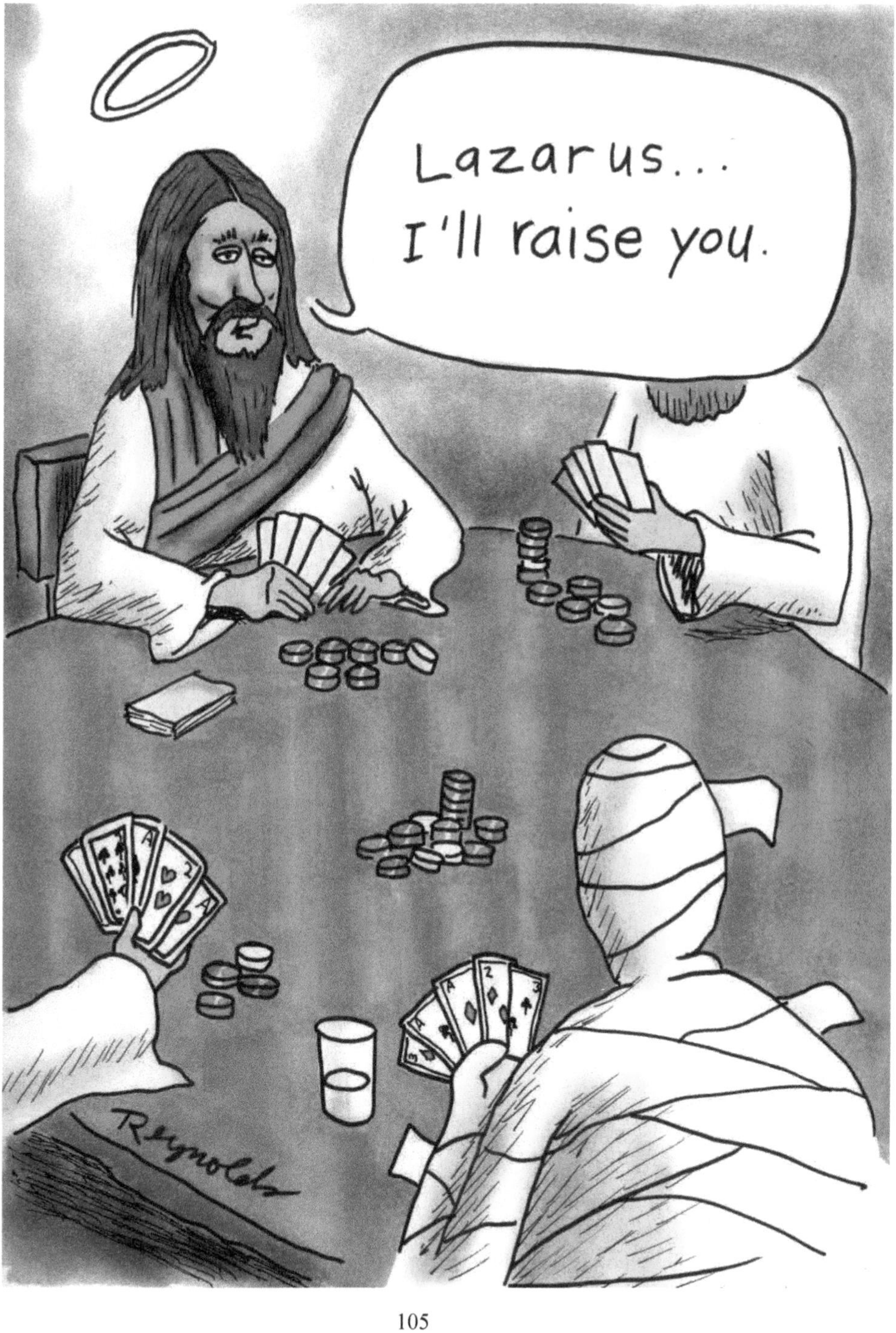
Lazarus...
I'll raise you.
Reynolds

Our loved ones in Heaven are NOT dead. They are more alive than we are because they are born to eternal life.

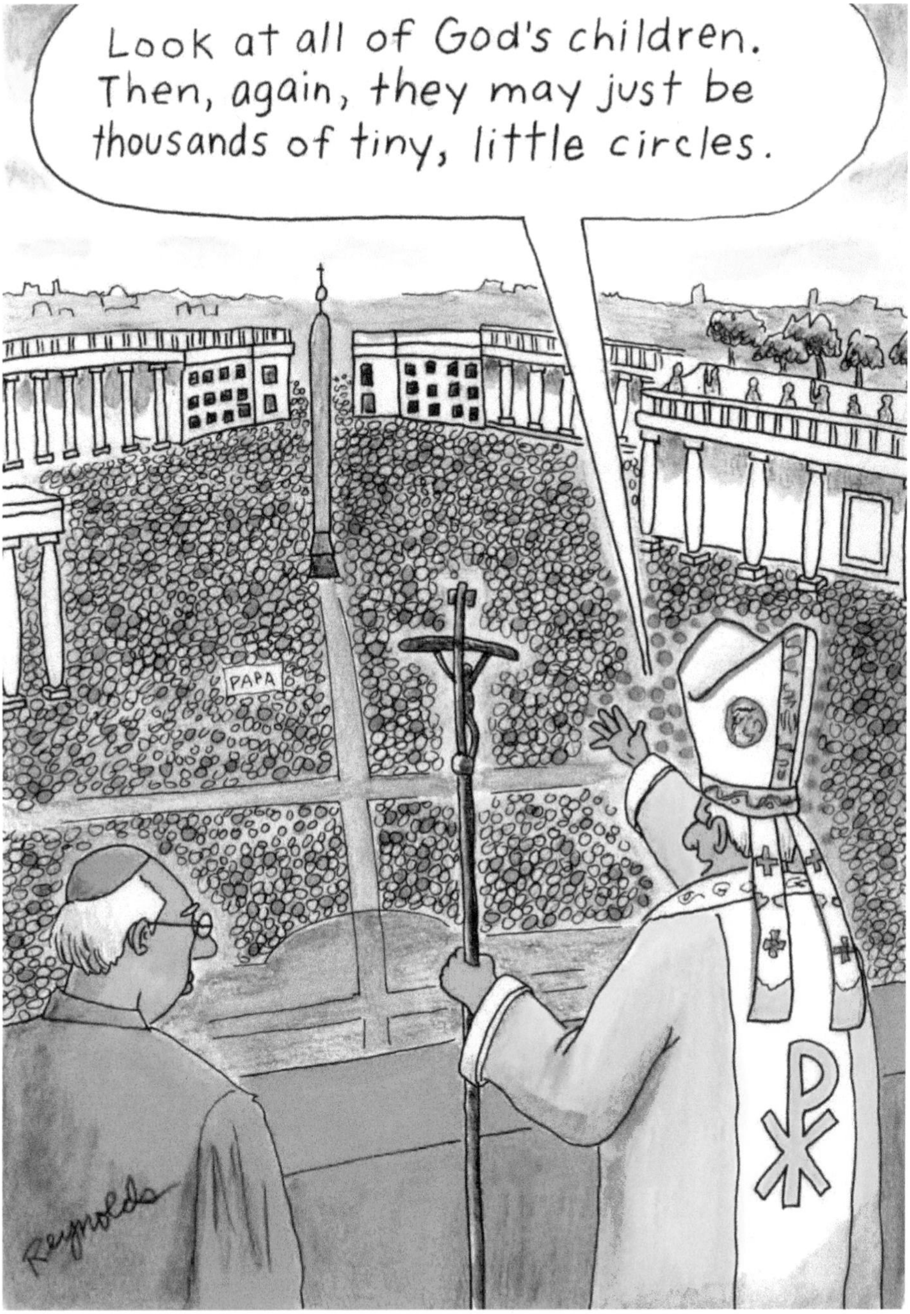
Look at all of God's children. Then, again, they may just be thousands of tiny, little circles.
PAPA
Reynolds

Karl Marx said, "Religion is the opiate of the masses". If this is true, it can only be because God is our Eternal "Poppy".

CONVENT SCHOOLS

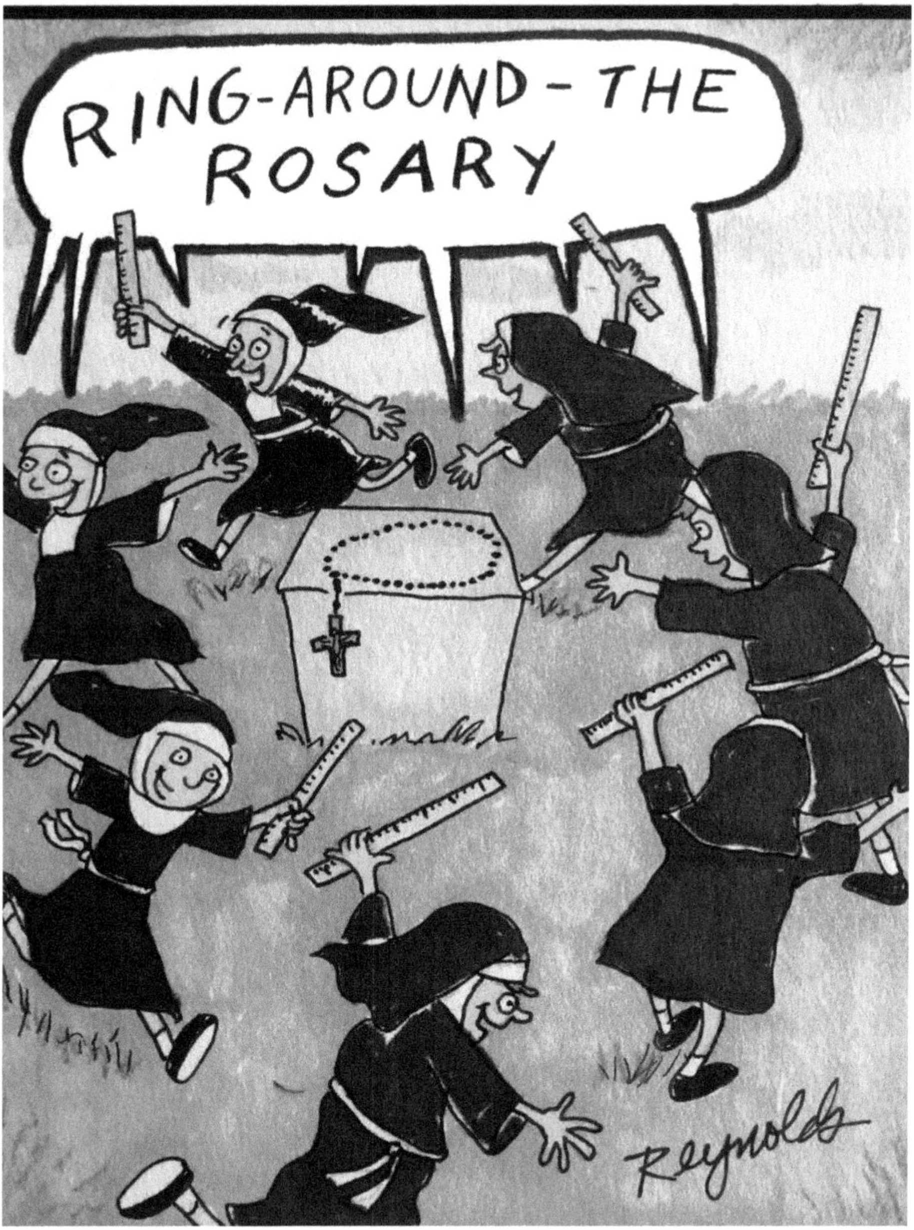
RING-AROUND-THE ROSARY
Reynolds

Ironically, the reason laughter is the best medicine is because it is infectious.

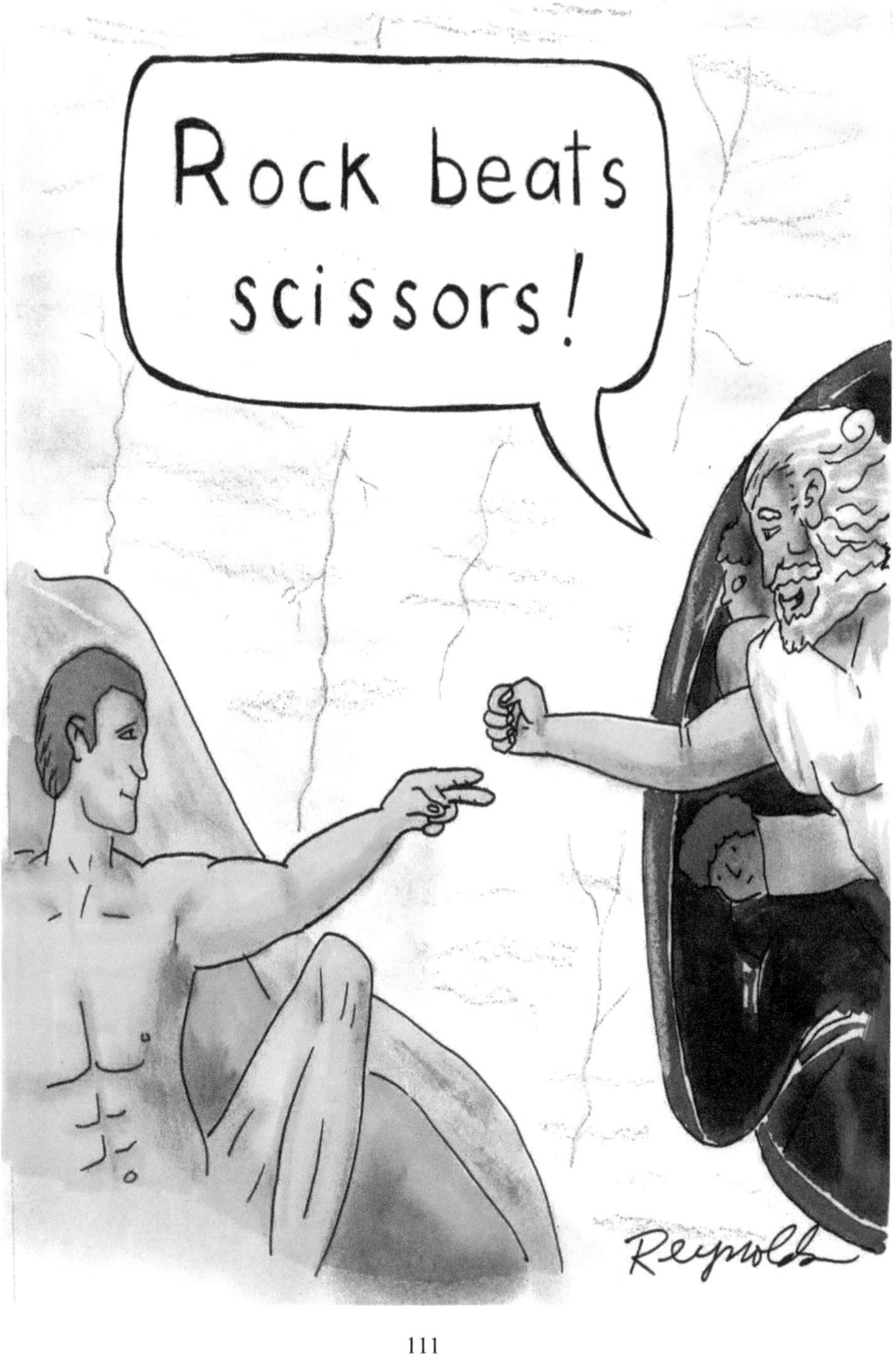
Rock beats scissors!
Reynolds

Just as we can only see our own reflection in still waters, we can see best God's reflection in ourselves when our hearts and minds are at peace.

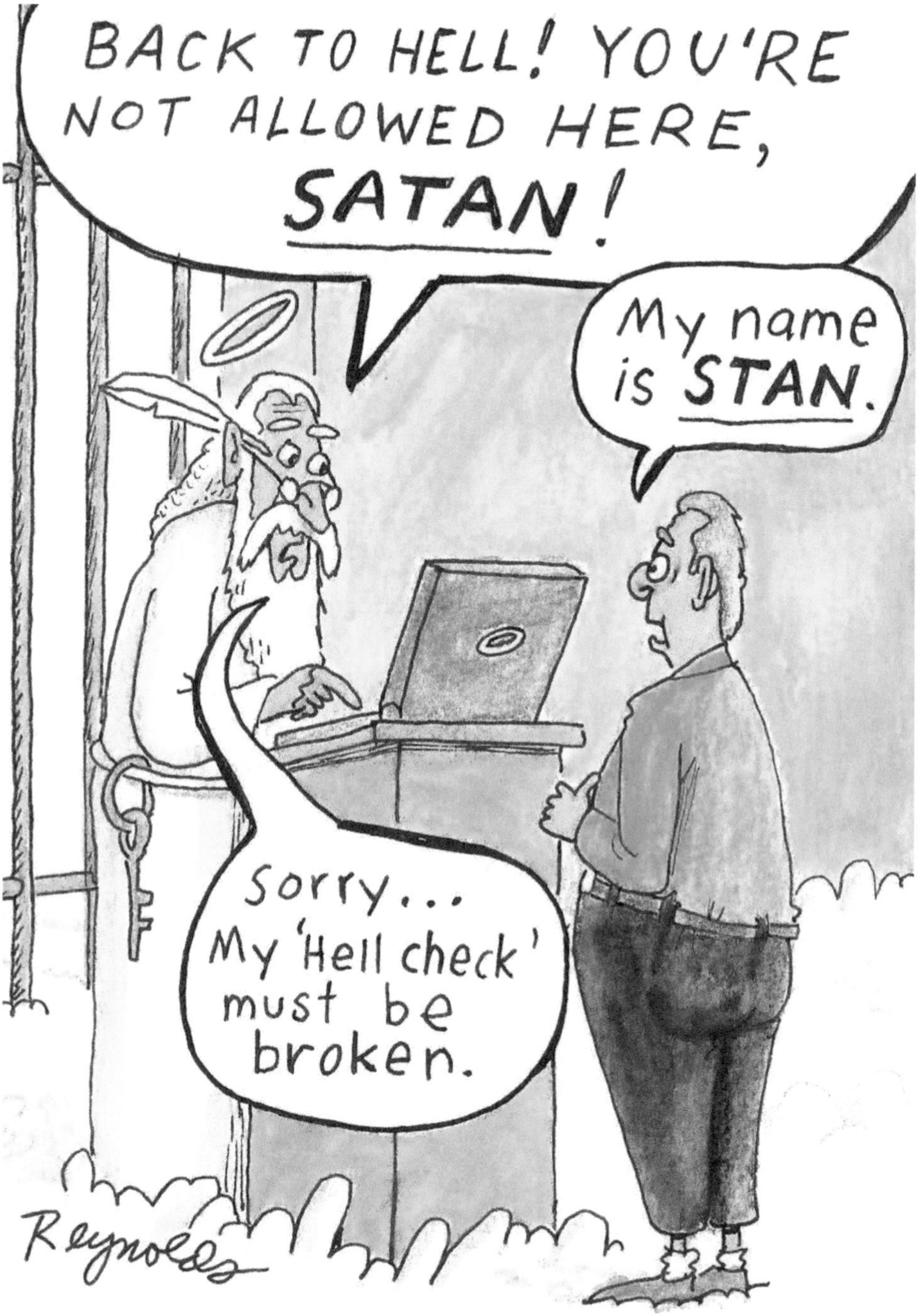
BACK TO HELL! YOU'RE NOT ALLOWED HERE, SATAN!
My name is STAN.
Sorry... My 'Hell check' must be broken.
Reynolds

God doesn't have an iPhone. He has an iAmPhone. If you turn your iPhone off and listen in silent prayer, you will hear Him constantly calling you.

"Mom and dad were right. We really do come from Heaven."

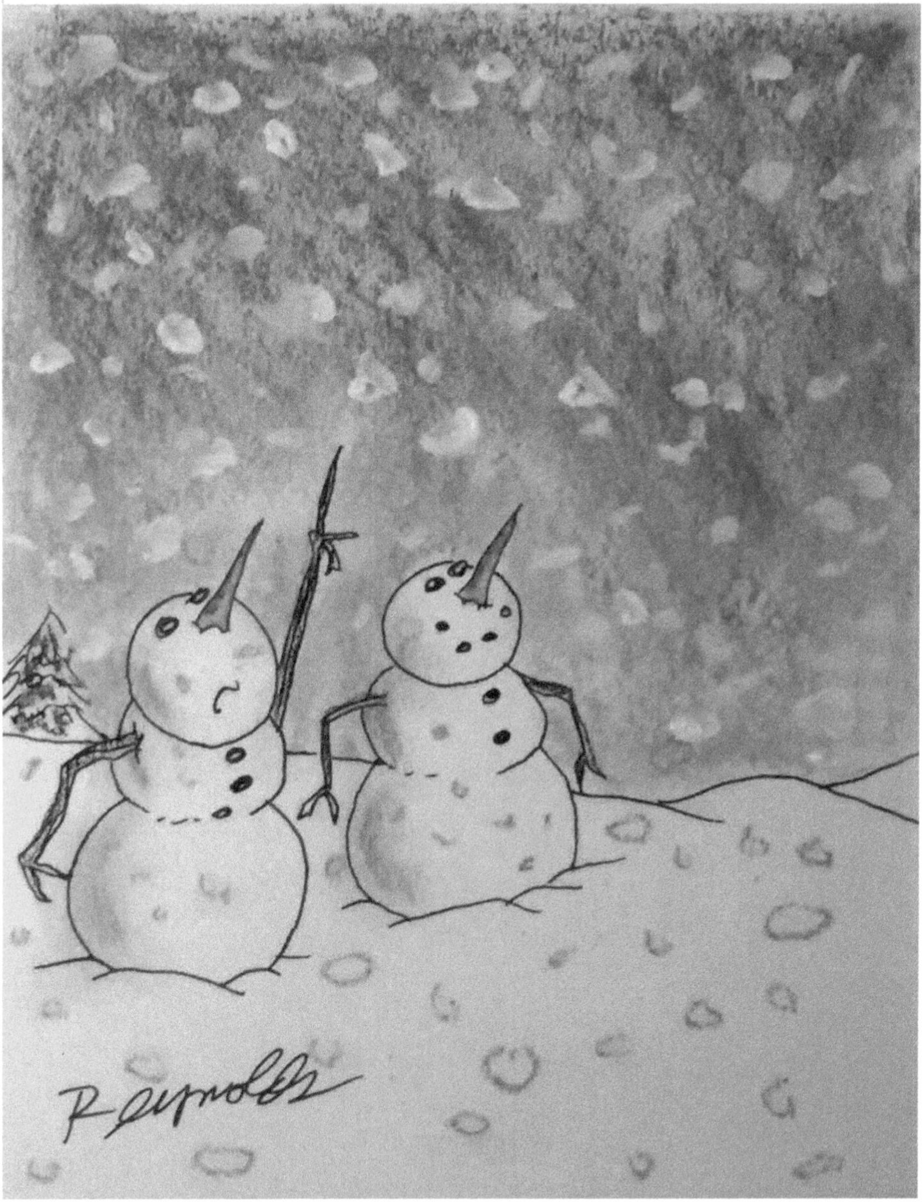

When I was a kid, every mother used her hand on their child's forehead to tell if they were running a temperature ...it was called: "Their Mom Meter".

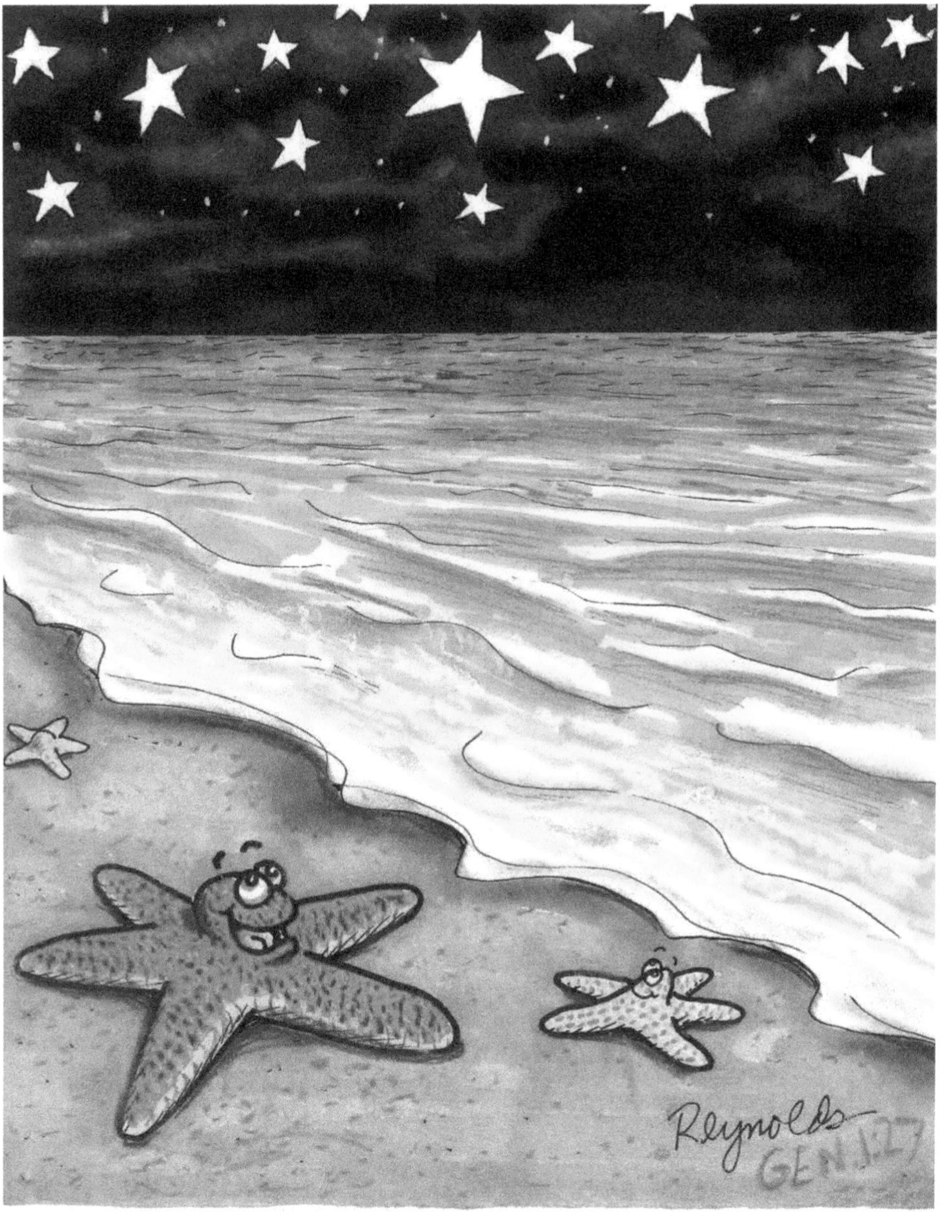
Reynolds
GEN 1:27

"You see, son, we are all made in <u>His</u> Image."

If in the Body of Christ, it turns out I was an elbow, that's fine with me.
It would be a glorious honor to be part of God's funny bone.

Dan Reynolds

Dan was born and raised a cradle Catholic in Oswego, NY. He attended Bishop Cunningham Catholic High School in Oswego, NY, graduated from SUNY Oswego with a degree in Psychology, spent 4 years in the Navy on the USS NIMITZ aircraft carrier traveling to many places in the world while working with the Navy Chaplains aboard the ship. He worked 22 years at the Oswego City County Youth Bureau as the Youth Activities Coordinator.

For the past 27 years, Dan has been a professional cartoonist. His cartoon work is distributed nationally via National Greeting card companies like American Greetings. His greeting card work can be found in every city in the country via outlets like Wal-Mart, Target, and many other chain stores. His work has also appeared in magazines like Reader's Digest, and Harvard Business Review, Boy's Life, Catholic Digest, and many others. Beginning in September of 2017, Dan's work will begin appearing in every issue of Catholic Digest. He has 4 nationally published books with Andrews McMeel Publishing, the publishers of Calvin and Hobbes and The Far Side.

His Reader's Digest artwork in a 4-month exhibit in 2011 at the Everson Museum in Syracuse, NY. His cartoon work also appeared once on an opening season episode of THE SOPRANOS, and on the Discovery's Science Channel. Two of his greeting cards won nominations for a LOUIE award. A LOUIE AWARD is the equivalent of the movie academy award nomination only in the greeting card industry.

Dan is a cancer survivor which he battled in 2008 and 2009, receiving chemo treatments along operations.

Currently, Dan is going into his second year of diaconate training for the Diocese of Syracuse, NY, having first completed the required preliminary 2 years of Formation for Ministry. God willing, Dan will be ordained a deacon in 2020.

When he's not cartooning, Dan's spends about 20 hours a week as the Coordinator of Parish Life at Divine Mercy Parish in Central Square, NY. And travels to share his apostolate THE DIVINE COMEDY presentation, hoping to spread the joy of the Gospel message.

And most importantly, Dan is married, and has 4 sons, (2 of which presently attend Franciscan University in Steubenville, Ohio), and lives in Brewerton, NY.

Dan's Divine Comedy website
and e-mail address is:
divinecomedydan@gmail.com
www.divinecomedydan.weebly.com

Sign-up for Dan's daily REYNOLDS
UNWRAPPED e-mail cartoon for only $12
for a whole year. E-mail Dan at
reynoldsunwrapped@gmail.com for
details. Dan's website is:
www.reynoldsunwrapped.weebly.com

The Funny Side Collection is available at:
www.thefunnysidecollection.com
www.smartaskbooks.com

CPSIA information can be obtained
at www.ICGtesting.com
Printed in the USA
LVHW022348071020
668276LV00005B/251